To Dellissima

Got a call from
Ron last summer
asking if I could
help him write
his book. I
enjoyed the process
of editing his
story. Hope you
enjoy reading about
his search.

brenda

POSSIBILITIES

A Search for Personal Liberation

DR. RONALD J. SHEEHY

iUniverse, Inc.
New York   Bloomington

Possibilities
A Search for Personal Liberation

All imagery courtesy of the author, with the exception of photographs in Tampa on pages 9, 16, and 29, by the Tampa Hillsborough County Public library System, Morehouse College photographs on pages 32, 34, 38 and 53, by the Morehouse Archive Office, the Oak Ridge Y-12 building on page 87, by the Oak Ridge National Laboratory Y-12 Archives, and the Public Health Research Building on page 89, by Google.

Cover designed by Phillip and Edwina Elliott

iUniverse books may be ordered through booksellers or by contacting:

iUniverse
1663 Liberty Drive
Bloomington, IN 47403
www.iuniverse.com
1-800-Authors (1-800-288-4677)

ISBN: 978-1-4502-2808-4 (pbk)
ISBN: 978-1-4502-2810-7 (cloth)
ISBN: 978-1-4502-2809-1 (ebook)

Printed in the United States of America

iUniverse rev. date: 5/27/10

To

Val and Marie, Franca, Ronald Jr., Lisa, Omari, and

Kwame, my grandchildren and great-grandchildren,

and to those yet to be born,

and to John Young, who believed in our cause.

CONTENTS

Acknowledgments

My love and gratitude for my parents, Val and Marie Sheehy, knows no bounds. I have tried to portray honestly the contributions of many individuals in this memoir. To all who helped me along the way, I owe a debt of gratitude. Brenda Crayton-Pitches, my excellent editor, dissipated the fog from my writing. My wife, Franca, soul mate and love of my life, provided support and critical insight during my writing.

To be unshackled,

to improve the mind,

to mold the character,

to dream dreams,

to develop the body,

to aspire to greatness,

or to strive for excellence

is the birthright of every child

born into the world.

And no society has the right

to smother ambition,

to curb motivation,

and to circumscribe the mind.

Dr. Benjamin E. Mays, 1894–1984
President Emeritus, Morehouse College

Prologue

In every society there are those who ask, "Why?" Our progress as humans, in every field of endeavor, depends on this critical consciousness. Our individual freedom is predicated on the exercise of this essential faculty. Following is a chronicle of the momentous events and the most important influences in my life. I was moved to write it because I want young people who, by their creativity, fearless exploration, undeterred search for truth, resistance to prejudice, and deep and abiding love for the Earth and its peoples, will grow up in a much better world. The goal is worthy of a lifetime of ardent pursuit.

I was taught not to believe in personal limitations, regardless of apparent obstacles or challenges. Life, I have come to understand, presents the possibilities of a creative response if we have the courage to respond. My life has been filled with improbable possibilities. Therefore, when I thought of a title for the memoir, *Possibilities* seemed an appropriate title. The subtitle, *A Search for Personal Liberation*, embodies the challenge to think critically and to have the courage of one's convictions. The subtitle also describes my individual struggle for self-expression during an era of change in this country that saw an expansion of civil and social rights.

The starting point for my journey was a profound belief in the benefits of education, a belief held by my grandparents and parents on both sides of my family. They believed in the transformative power of education. Combined with hard work, education could lead a person to a successful, productive future. My parents lived and worked in a period when opportunities for black Americans were restricted and controlled by law and custom. They knew the perils of an unbridled curiosity, which might be life-threatening in the oppressive and stifling environment of the American South. Yet I was encouraged to explore, to question, and to investigate. At an early age, I developed an interest in science. In college, I found a mentor who encouraged me to think critically, to analyze and evaluate, and to challenge assumptions. My exposure to critical thinking was congruent with the philosophical values of another major mentor, Dr. Benjamin E. Mays, the president of Morehouse College, who preached that academic excellence and the courage to follow one's convictions were prerequisites for individual empowerment. These ideas emphasized at Morehouse inspired Martin Luther King Jr., a Morehouse graduate, and influenced and liberated my thinking as well.

The first usage of the term *Morehouse man* is probably lost to history. However, beyond designation of Morehouse graduates, the transcendent term provided validation, empowerment, and an alternative identity, an antidote to the pejorative and ambiguous term *Negro*. A Morehouse man was as valued in the black community as the Harvard man was in the majority community. President Mays and his faculty set high standards and challenged all graduates to become leaders, to confront injustice, and to be examples of the best that the black community could offer. It is no small wonder that, in spite of its size and resources, this college has contributed disproportionately, through its graduates, to the ideals of freedom and democracy in this nation and the world.

While the foundation was laid by my parents, my life's overall shape emerged from the crucible of Morehouse. The values I learned as a student at Morehouse, and then practiced as a teacher and scientist there, contributed to my philosophical outlook. The journey led me into a world, succinctly described here, of scientific exploration. It is my fervent desire that my story will be a catalyst to prompt parents, teachers, and students to reexamine their general approaches to education and to realize the emancipating benefits of approaching life in a lively spirit of intellectual criticism.

I urge parents to encourage reading and make sure that their children achieve a fundamental understanding of mathematics and science, which will provide them with the ability to interpret the world. Provide a nurturing environment that fosters creativity, inventiveness, and exploration. Children are capable of being creative if parents allow their attributes to flourish.

I urge teachers to treat students as partners and collaborators in the learning process. Respect youthful opinions, resist authoritarianism, promote dialogue, encourage deep analysis and inquiry, and become a problem-posing facilitator who stimulates true reflection rather than a deliverer of facts to be memorized.

I urge students not to become mere repositories for information, but to examine, question, and challenge assumptions critically so they can arrive at their own conclusions. Hone the capacity to evaluate skillfully, weigh evidence, and detect hypocrisy and manipulation. The process has been termed "critical thinking" and leads to personal liberation.

From my account of my experiences, perhaps you will be inspired on your own journey toward personal liberation.

Foundations: Family

— 1 —

Joseph Valentine "Val" Sheehy

In a very special place in my mother's house, there hangs a photographic enlargement of a picture of my dad in his Army uniform. Although he was a serious man who smiled reluctantly, his smile in that picture is contagious. He was relatively tall, more than six feet, with straight black hair. His brown skin accentuated a mustache line just above his lip, in the style of the day.

Joseph Valentine Sheehy was very proud of the fact that he served his country in World War II. In a reflective mood, he would recall, "I managed to get one of the highest scores on the Army's officer training test, only to be denied admission to officer training school because of my race."

Val, as his friends called him, returned home with the rank of master sergeant, but he never forgot the injustice of being denied access to officer training. I thought it remarkable that he wanted to serve his country at a time when blacks were denied full citizenship at home. His, of course, was not an unusual story. Countless numbers of blacks of his generation heeded the call to fight for liberty and to prove their ability to serve as soldiers as well as their white counterparts.

Marie "Dollar" Hart

My mother's first name is Marie, but her friends have always known her as "Dollar" because of her ability to hang onto a dollar bill tightly. Her maiden name was Hart; people in her family were not endowed with great stature, and my mother was the shortest among her siblings. She was also the feistiest among them, and she had a striking figure and slightly bowed legs. She grew up on the east side of Jacksonville, Florida, in a working class white neighborhood.

The Harts were the only black family in their neighborhood. Although Jacksonville was a segregated southern town, the Harts were accorded a special status. The legend is that because my mother's grandfather was white, the Harts were allowed to live in the neighborhood.

One Christmas, however, Klansmen in the area lost historical memory of the arrangement and burned a cross in the front yard. My grandfather made a phone call, which ended the cross burnings in the yard. He apparently knew influential whites who interceded on his behalf. These stories are not particular to my parents, but represent the milieu and challenge of living while black in the south before the civil rights movement. Opportunity was circumscribed by legal statute and custom, and gratuitous violence was a part of the landscape.

My grandfather, Stephen Coneval Hart, known in the family as "Papa," was an industrious, hardworking, church-going man. He stood about five feet tall, shaved his head, and always wore suspenders and a belt. In spite of his short stature, he was always in control. For years Papa was superintendent of the Sunday school and deacon in charge of finances of the church. If the preacher ran afoul of my grandfather, the preacher would have to go. He also was a foreman at Gulf Oil, a refinery in Jacksonville, and he prided himself on his ability to secure jobs for his friends. He had a quiet resolve that emanated from his steadfast belief in the Bible, which he read constantly. He gave no speeches. Papa's strength and fortitude did not require words.

In 1865 his mother, Lucy Hart, contributed to the establishment of the oldest African Methodist Episcopal (AME) church in Florida, Midway AME. Blacks who worked in the nearby lumber mills lived in an area located midway between Jacksonville and New Berlin, Florida. The settlement, Midway, derived its name from this location. It was also home to members of the Robinson family, who contributed to the founding of the church. Legend says that the church was burned down by the Klan and rebuilt, in 1921, in East Jacksonville, where it is located today. Every year the church, now known as "Mother Midway," celebrates its founding and commemorates Hart-Robinson Day.

My grandmother, Alberta Luvenia Hart (whom we called Berta Hart), was a housewife, and she was the quiet, reassuring backbone of the family. Berta Hart believed in the value of education and pushed her children to excel in school.

Her mother, a diminutive woman known as "Granny Rosa," was born into slavery. Unlike my grandmother, she was an independent-minded, liberated woman who had several husbands, traveled incessantly, gave birth to more than twenty children, taught school, and could drink and smoke with the best of men. Not surprisingly, she and her son-in-law, my grandfather, did not see eye-to-eye. Also unsurprisingly, my mother looked up to Granny Rosa and admired her spunk. Granny Rosa lived to be more than a hundred years old, and when my mother and I were in Jacksonville, we always visited her.

My mother had three siblings: Johnny, Henry, and Paralee. Because my grandfather insisted that church music was the only respectable music, the Hart siblings' talents for singing and playing the piano were underdeveloped, though they had the potential to become professional musicians. Education became a substitute for music as a career; all three graduated from college, and all three became teachers.

Part of our family lore is that Val, Dollar, and Paralee, my mother's sister, were first acquainted when they worked as teachers with two-year degrees in the general vicinity of Marianna, Florida. In those days, one could teach with only two years of college.

Marianna, the county seat of Jackson County, was the hub of commerce in an area located near the Alabama border in the panhandle of Florida. The local county establishment provided minimal educational opportunities for the black children whose parents picked beans and cotton in the fields. The schools, located in rural areas, were one-room facilities with one or two teachers. Paralee and Dollar taught in the schools and lived with an elderly woman who took in boarders from time to time. Val, one of the eligible bachelors in the area and principal at one of the schools, walked miles from his home to visit the two sisters. He sat and engaged in small talk without allowing either to know whom he preferred. As the story goes, the landlady said to Dollar, "That sure is a fine gentleman that comes to see ya'll. I wonder who he's pining for?"

Dollar replied, "Aw, he's too much of a gentleman to reveal his feelings."

After months, when the question of Val's preference still appeared unresolved, Val finally confessed to Dollar at a picnic that she was the girl of his choice, prompting the landlady to ask, "Why does he like that little one? The other seems more his type."

War interrupted the relationship. When Val returned after the war, he was determined to complete his college education, and he finished his last two years at North Carolina Central University in Durham, North Carolina. During wartime, Dollar attended Tuskegee Institute in Tuskegee, Alabama. At the time, Tuskegee was also the site of a "military experiment" to train black pilots. Pilots who were trained in the experiment are now known, famously, as the Tuskegee Airmen. Acts of bravery and courage by the cadre of young black pilots trained at Tuskegee have been officially recognized by the United States government.

Dollar would recall, with unabashed pride, "I had never seen so many fine black men in one place. They would come around dressed in their aviator uniforms and sweep the girls off their feet."

Marie (Dollar)
with Tuskegee Airman

Turning the pages of my mother's album of photographs taken during those days at Tuskegee, I am struck by how young, vibrant, and attractive she looks, along with the young pilot-in-training who posed with her. Of course, the obligatory smiles are for the camera, but underneath the smiles and apparent frivolity is the stark reality of expectation and peril. Soldiers in the pictures would witness untold horrors, and large numbers would not return from war.

Dollar graduated from Tuskegee in 1944 with a Bachelor of Arts degree and returned to Jacksonville, Florida, to resume her career as a teacher. Shortly thereafter, she met a young, college-educated bachelor, John Thompson. He was so "good-looking," she would tell me. John had graduated with a degree in chemistry from Florida A & M University, in Tallahassee, Florida. He wanted to become a physician; however, a congenital eye disease, which limited his sight, short-circuited both a career in medicine and service in the military. He taught school for a few years after college, worked on trains as a Pullman porter for a while, and eventually became a medical technician.

"John was your father," my mother recounts with simple sincerity. "Your grandmother, Mattie Thompson, loved you dearly and wanted us to marry, but things didn't work out between me and her son." Although John Thompson was my biological father, he played no significant role in my life.

I was born in 1945, and my earliest recollections are of toddling around in my Grandpa and Grandma Hart's house in Jacksonville, Florida. I have a faint memory of Val, on occasional visits, and the toys that he brought. A tricycle that he gave me looms large in my fond memories of my childhood years. I remember his attention as genuine, a feeling that was reinforced over and over as we shared our lives together.

Dad (Val) Mom and Me

Foundations: Tampa

— 2 —

Dollar and Val were married, and we moved to Tampa, Florida, around 1950. We moved into three rooms that Val built with his own hands. He added one room at a time until we had a five-room bungalow.

Dad (Val) with hammer

At the time, Tampa was comparable to other towns and cities in the South. Rigid segregation was legal, with black and white water fountains, black and white movie theatres, and black and white schools and neighborhoods. A small Hispanic community, mostly of Cuban descent, was divided between two areas of town: West Tampa and Ybor City. Val's family, the Sheehys, lived and worked among the Cubans in West Tampa. His Irish grandfather and West Indian grandmother lived in West Tampa as husband and wife.

Both of my parents had one white grandparent. This fact is not remarkable for black families in this country; however, in both instances, a white man not only sired children with a black woman but also lived with her as her husband despite the legal prohibition against interracial marriage.

My dad's father, Joe Sheehy, owned a butcher shop in West Tampa, spoke Spanish, and moved easily between the black and Cuban communities. Although Joe and his wife, Anna-Loraine Sheehy, were not college-educated, they insisted that their children receive a first-class education at the Catholic schools in Tampa. Of the seven siblings, three girls and three boys earned a college degree. The group produced one physician, three teachers, two school principals (Val being one), and one homemaker.

My dad spoke a bit of Spanish, but he was not as closely associated with the Cubans as his dad. However, I remember the respect he received from the Cubans in the community, particularly when we visited the Alessi bakery on Saturday mornings.

"Cómo está, Professor Sheehy?"

"Muy bien, gracias," my dad would answer.

Afterwards, a conversation in Spanish continued until we finalized the purchase of Cuban bread and pastries. On frequent Saturday mornings, we visited my dad's favorite coffee diner, the Greek Stand. It was located in the hub of the black business district in Tampa, on the corner of Scott and Central Avenues. I recall one such Saturday.

"What's up, Prof?" This was the usual greeting from an elderly black man behind the counter. He had an unshaven gray beard and an apron that needed to be washed. "How about some of that dishwater you call coffee?" my dad joked.

"Who is that with you?" "This is my son, Ronald." "Fine-looking little fellow. What do you want to do when you grow up?" I always answered, "I want to be a teacher like my dad."

The Greek Stand on the corner of Scott and Central Avenues

"Prof, why don't you school your son? Teachers don't make any money. Son, you need to think of being an athlete, like Jackie Robinson, or a singer, like Ray Charles."

I wonder how the proprietor would have responded if I had answered, "I want to be a scientist." I'm guessing, but that conversation might have continued, "What kind of occupation is that for a Negro?"

With the exceptions of sports and entertainment, occupations beyond the black norm during those times were generally considered out of black Americans' reach.

The way my dad moved between black and Cuban cultures in Tampa was reminiscent of his dad's way of life. He respected people regardless of their culture or economic position. He was clear that we should be proud of our family name and accomplishments, but he let us know that we should not think ourselves superior to anyone because we had a little more. In order to drive that point home, he took me to visit an old black man who lived under the North Boulevard Street Bridge. At a time when homelessness was rare, someone who had built a house of cardboard and wood under a bridge was a most unusual sight. To prepare for our visit, we gathered canned goods and various food items for the old man. As we approached his shack, a figure emerged, dressed mostly in rags and barely recognizable as a human being. Surprisingly, the man was not ignorant and spoke in complete sentences. He must have suffered from a mental condition, but he recognized my dad immediately.

"Professor Sheehy, is that you?"

My dad answered, "You old coot, I see you are still alive."

"I'll be here until this bridge falls on me," he said defiantly, with a bemused chuckle. We were invited to join him inside; however, my dad politely turned down the invitation.

"Do you remember my son, Ronald?"

"Yep, I see he's growing. I've been fishing in the river, would you like to share some of this?"

"No, thank you," my dad said gently, with care not to appear embarrassed at the thought of accepting food from him.

Toward the end of our visit, we gave the old man the canned goods and other items. He thanked us for our visit and watched as we retraced our path around the pilings and up a narrow path that led back to the road where we had parked. I cannot remember a lecture on the golden rule; however, I am certain that, by his example, Dad wanted me to feel compassion and empathy for individuals who are less fortunate. He made his point.

The Golden Rule of Christianity is often expressed as "Do unto others as you would have them do onto you." In most religions, a version of the Golden Rule is incorporated in the religious doctrine. The idea that all humans are equal in importance and should be treated in a decent manner was fundamental to my dad's philosophical outlook.

Foundations: School Days

Ronald Sheehy, six years old

By a quirk of fate, or a doting teacher aunt who carried me to school with her, I completed the first grade at the age of four in Jacksonville. When we moved to Tampa, my parents enrolled me in second grade at Dunbar Elementary, only a brief walk from our house.

Plenty of kids lived in the neighborhood, and although my parents were teachers—a middle-class occupation in the black community—I didn't consider myself better off than my playmates. When we purchased the first television in the neighborhood, I felt a little different from my playmates, but I was glad to share, and the kids gathered at our house in the afternoon to watch the couple of hours of available programming. In many ways, the neighborhood was idyllic despite the segregation. The resourcefulness of the black community was evident on various levels. We lived on Main Street, which was the major thoroughfare in West Tampa. Anthony's Drive Inn was on our block, and there one could get an excellent milk shake and a hamburger. This eatery, developed by a black entrepreneur, was a major innovation in the Tampa area. It was domed-shaped, and its outer exterior was stainless steel.

In the next block were Frog's Grocery Store and Maddox's Barbershop. Further up the block was a confectionary where kids hung out. Even further were more small businesses, a beauty shop, and a gas station. At the end of the street was our neighborhood theatre, the Carver Theatre. Hardly any crime existed, and schools were within walking distance of homes. Occasionally the black Free Masons, a separately chartered group from the white Free Masons, established by Prince Hall and fourteen other freed slaves in 1784, and the Lilly White Association, a women's suffrage group, would stage a parade down Main Street.

When I wasn't playing with the neighborhood kids, I spent time with my dog, Fuzzy Wuzzy. He was a crossbreed of collie and golden retriever. How I loved that dog! When we visited my grandparents in Jacksonville, he went right along. We shared a room; my room was his room. When I left for school, he was released into the yard, with no fence. Fuzzy Wuzzy waited by the side door for me to return home and never wandered off. Main Street was a busy thoroughfare, with considerable traffic. His one fault was to chase cars. One day he got a little too close to a car that he chased and was run over. I immediately ran from my yard and into the street. As I attempted to drag him from the street, another car barely missed me. He died in my arms. I will never forget the smell of torn flesh and blood-drenched hair, and I took a while to recover from the ordeal. My mother attempted to introduce me to other dogs, but none compared to Fuzzy Wuzzy. Every kid should grow up with a pet. If close, the relationship teaches friendship, empathy, compassion, and respect for both animals and humans.

My mother was a devoted educator and reading specialist. She bragged that she could teach any kid to read.

"If you can't read," she regularly admonished me, "you can't do anything."

She had learned to read because she wanted to emulate her older brothers, who could read. "I never wanted to be outdone by my brothers," she still says today. "I read to you constantly, even when you were two years old," she tells me. "Then I taught you the alphabet and how to associate the alphabet with simple words. I showed you pictures so you could associate pictures with words. I would call out the sounds of words, and you would associate the sounds with the words. Books were everywhere. When we took trips, you took two or three books to read. By the time you were four, you were reading, and I credit this method with your desire to read now."

In the third grade, I was an undersized six-year-old. Perhaps, to give me a chance to catch up physically, my parents thought that I should repeat the third grade as a student in my mother's third grade class at College Hill Elementary. The arrangement seemed to work, even though my personality as an active child had emerged. However, when I was promoted to fourth grade, Mrs. Gibson, the fourth grade teacher, did not go along with the program. One of the best teachers in the school, Mrs. Gibson insisted on strict decorum in her classroom.

"Ronald, you are going to have to sit still in this classroom. This is not your mother's classroom. If you don't stop talking, I'm goin' to whip your little butt!"

I couldn't sit still in class. I was up and down, out of my seat, and into everything except paying attention to Mrs. Gibson. In our contemporary school environment, I probably would have been diagnosed as hyperactive and prescribed a serious dose of Ritalin. My mother could have made the argument that I needed to be engaged in a manner different from Mrs. Gibson's approach. She would have been onto something, as educators have come to realize. The suppression of creativity, inventiveness, and exploration can be byproducts of a strict disciplinary approach. On the other hand, Mrs. Gibson would have responded that I was not special. After all, she had a class full of children with different needs. I simply needed to behave. My first brush with an authoritarian, no-nonsense personality type would not be my last, and the scenario would reoccur throughout my life. Since that time, I have concluded that, in the name of discipline, countless teachers are more absorbed in the preservation of their authority in the classroom rather than in encouraging inventiveness, curiosity, and questioning.

My parents concluded that keeping me in Mrs. Gibson's classroom was not worth the fight and decided that I should attend Carver Elementary School, where my dad was the principal. Moreover, I was placed in fifth grade, essentially undoing the decision to hold me back in third grade. After the decision, I was eight years old and in the fifth grade.

My school life was significantly altered by the transition. I entered a new school at midyear, and my classmates were two and three years older. I managed to do the work in class but was out of place socially. I was two years ahead of my peer group, shorter than average, and probably looked as though I should be in kindergarten rather than fifth grade.

Carver was a friendly environment, notwithstanding my father's position as principal. The neighborhood school was populated with students from government-subsidized housing, known as the "projects," only a block away. At that time, living in the projects held no stigma because blacks of all backgrounds and occupations lived, or were segregated, within the same geographical area.

I remember an incident that was rather unsettling. My dad had disciplined a female student in his office. Perhaps he used some sort of corporal punishment. In any event, the girl told her brothers of the incident, and a mob formed after school to deal with my dad. I stood on the sidewalk and watched as the menacing group threatened my dad.

"Come out of that office," the leader of the mob yelled. "If you want to punish somebody, come out and punish me," he hollered at the top of his voice.

The mob started to shout in unison, "Come out! Come out!"

Fortunately my dad did not come out of his office, and the crowd eventually went away. Because of the incident, students started to refer to my dad as "Shane," after a popular character in a cowboy movie. My dad was a no-nonsense principal, but he did not deserve the unflattering "gunslinger" nickname. In fact, if they had known the fights my dad waged on behalf of the school, those students would have had a different opinion. He constantly beseeched the school administration for books and modern equipment for his school. Dad, like Papa, was soft-spoken and strong-willed.

An incident that involved the superintendent is illustrative. The superintendent decided that he needed cuts of meat for a private function. He sent one of his people to ask my dad to donate the meat from the school cafeteria. My dad refused and lectured the intermediary about school property that he didn't have the authority to give away. Within a few weeks, my dad's job was threatened. He was moved from Carver to a smaller school. His sense of responsibility and character would not allow him to break the law or yield indiscriminately to authority.

In 1954, the U.S. Supreme Court decided, in the case *Brown versus Board of Education*, that segregation in public schools was illegal and declared that "separate educational facilities are inherently unequal." During the early part of the 1950s before the ruling, states and cities in the South sought to upgrade schools in the black community as part of a strategy to forestall integration. The separate-but-equal doctrine was under attack, and school officials sought to placate the black community with a message that separate could be equal with the addition of a few new schools in the community.

While fervently sought by the civil rights establishment, the prospect of integration was not taken for granted by my parents, particularly my dad. I remember discussions of this landmark decision. As he sat at the kitchen table, my dad tilted his head as though he could see into the distance and asked philosophically, "Who is going to be concerned about the education of black children if we integrate? What's going to happen to black principals and black teachers? Will we keep our jobs? Will they take the best black teachers and transfer them to white schools?" My dad was not a segregationist but a practical-minded man, thoroughly familiar with the South and the power relations between blacks and whites. Numerous unanswered questions filled his thoughts. He understood the argument that black children were disadvantaged in segregated schools; however, his more fundamental concern was related to questions of leadership in schools. As educational institutions were integrated, beginning in the 1960s and beyond, in Tampa and communities throughout the nation, his concerns were not unfounded.

Howard W. Blake High School

Our new black-only high school, Howard W. Blake, was a modern brick structure situated on the shores of a bend in the Hillsborough River. Opened in 1956, it was named for a prominent black educator in Tampa. Everything there was new except the textbooks, which were hand-me-downs from the white schools. The school was a combination high school and junior high school, which began at grade seven. The administrative and teaching staff consisted of a blend of veteran teachers and new teachers who brought vitality and progressive ideas. I was in the first seventh grade class, and the challenge to adapt was stressful. My classmates knew that I was younger than they were, yet they included me in all of their activities. I slowly adjusted to the new environment.

Blake was also a vocational school as well as a college preparatory school. Therefore students were assigned either to a college preparatory track or a vocational track. I was placed in the college preparatory track. I joined the marching and concert bands, played clarinet, and began to dream of a career in music. The possibility waned pretty quickly. Although I was an enthusiastic participant in band activities, I was only an average clarinet player. I even tried out for the chorus, but failing the audition dashed my hopes of a singing career. Since music would not be prominent in my future, I looked to other disciplines. I wanted to become an expert in something. After I had read *War and Peace*, Tolstoy's great novel of nineteenth-century Russia, I dreamt of being a Russian scholar. I was becoming a romantic and fantasized about the time I would meet a girl like Natasha, the heroine in the novel. I remember the time as one of the happiest and contented of my life. My imagination, filled with a future of adventure and exploration, was fertile. My parents were not overbearing and allowed me to succeed or fail on my own terms. Importantly, they encouraged my constant questioning. They understood the fundamental importance of the searching curiosity of children. The need to inquire about the world around us drives our first strivings as human beings.

A Friend Indeed

— 4 ——————————————————————————

I met Victor Buchannan in the ninth grade. We were in the same homeroom. His face was narrow and angular, topped off with a short afro. Long gangly arms were attached to broad shoulders. He was at least twice my height. After school we loved to play on the adjacent playground. When his time came to choose a team, he always picked me. I returned the favor, and we became quite a force on the court. Victor lived across the street from the high school, in the projects. He lived with his mother, little brother, and sister in a sparsely furnished two-bedroom apartment.

Several classmates thought he was a bit eccentric and teased him. Initially, basketball drew us together. However, one day Victor invited me to his apartment to show me his telescope. At first I thought he was kidding, but I soon discovered that he had a very powerful telescope that could discern details on the moon, planets, and various objects in the night sky. I was not only fascinated by his telescope; we shared a curiosity about things scientific. Victor decided to develop a two-stage rocket, which he would launch from his yard in front of the high school. While I supported my friend, I thought the idea was pretty bold. On occasion he showed us aluminum canisters he had designed for the rocket, which elicited more derision and chuckles from our classmates.

I persuaded my parents to buy a telescope for me. However, they did not invest in one as expensive as Victor's. Victor's mother, who was barely getting by, had encouraged his interest in science and had bought a top-of-the-line telescope for his explorations.

Whether at my house or Victor's, we stayed up late to look into the night sky. My parents always treated Victor like one of the family. On occasions we set our telescopes up in a lot across the street from my house on Main Street. Because we were on a well-traveled street, we attracted the curiosity of a variety of people, including the neighborhood drunks who stumbled past us.

"Hey, little Negroes, what you boys got there?" asked an inebriated fellow.

"These are telescopes, and we're watching craters on the moon," Victor answered, hoping the men would continue on and leave us alone.

"Let me see," the most curious one said. We felt powerless and moved out of the way. As he positioned himself closer to the telescope, he said, "I don't see squat. You boys are crazy." He had actually looked into the wrong end of the telescope. Once we showed him the correct way to use it, he was satisfied and moved along.

With the exception of this kind of excitement, we were left to ourselves. To stay up until four or five in the morning was not unusual. We were awed by the craters on the moon, the rings of Saturn, the luminescence of Venus, and the vast numbers of star formations that we studied and identified. We talked about possibilities of travel to the moon, space travel, and going back in time. We imagined ourselves beyond the segregated community in which we were consigned and embraced the cosmos as an environment more accessible than the movie theatre downtown.

The following quote has been on my desk for years. "In every society there is always one who asks, why?" At an early age, my friend Victor was endowed with the spirit of inquiry and exploration.

Too many young people want to be creative and to experiment but are often discouraged. Society pays a price in ideas that are lost from suppressed inventiveness and the demand for conformity. Problems that appear intractable are not solved, and the individual loses the chance to contribute his or her creative talent.

The Science Fair

**We all have possibilities we don't know about. We
can do things we don't even dream we can do.**

Dale Carnegie

Mr. Roland Yates

We are often influenced in our lives by
individuals, particularly teachers, and by
their sheer force of personality, they can
change our prospects for the future. Mr.
Roland Yates, my tenth grade science
teacher, fits the description. A graduate
of Talledega College in Talledega,
Alabama, Mr. Yates was hired to teach
science at Blake. He brought unbounded
enthusiasm to his job and made science
fun to study. While I enjoyed his class,
he encouraged us to pursue an interest
in science outside of class and to develop
projects to enter in the competitive science fair sponsored by the City
of Tampa. Both white and black schools were invited to participate
in the competition. The fact that we were competing with white

students in such a direct way was unusual, given the practices of strict segregation within the schools.

Victor and I explored all kinds of possible projects. I scoured popular science magazines for ideas and finally found one that caught my interest. I decided to demonstrate the production of electricity from solar heat. That article's author persuaded me that conversion of solar heat into electricity would be important eventually, even though energy was abundant and available at modest cost at that time. Moreover, I hoped this kind of project would catch the attention of the science fair judges.

The how-to article described the use of two metals to create a thermocouple which, when heated, would produce a small electrical current. The feature described the way to organize pairs of the metal wires in an arrangement on an asbestos plate. When a wire was heated at one end, sufficient current was produced at the other end to drive the propeller of a small model plane engine. The heat was supplied by a solar panel to concentrate sun rays into a beam.

"What a great project," I thought. My challenge was to procure all the parts. The article provided a list of mail order companies that stocked the parts, with the exception of the model plane engine. I discovered that the model plane engine of a specific size and voltage requirement was available in toy stores. Consumed by the project, I rushed home every afternoon to see if the parts had been delivered.

Since the model plane engine could be found at a toy store, I reasoned that the toy store a few miles from school might have it. After school one day, I decided to walk to the store. A few blocks past the school, I made a left turn on North Boulevard, a main thoroughfare. I walked across the North Boulevard Street Bridge, which reminded me of the homeless old man, through unfamiliar neighborhoods, and a few miles to the store. I arrived in the late afternoon and was told that the store did not carry the specific model engine. However, the clerk informed me of a store that specialized in model plane engines. That store was a few miles away. I decided to continue to the specialty store. I arrived well after dark. The clerk said I had made it in the nick of time; they were closing for the day.

I described the model plane engine, and he said they had one in stock. He inquired where I lived. When I told him, "West Tampa," he said I was at least ten miles away from my home. He wondered how I would get home and volunteered to call my mother, who drove there to pick me up.

Since that time, I have thought about the compelling desire that propelled me that afternoon. I was not conscious of the distance I had walked or the time of day. I was lost in the task, and time had vanished. Passion and intensity are often needed to take on difficult tasks.

With all the parts at hand, my task was to see if a good theoretical idea actually worked in practice. A friend, an upperclassman in a radio class, agreed to help align the thermocouple wires on the asbestos board according to specifications in the article. Afterwards we tested the board, connecting the wires to my small model plane engine with the propeller. We heated the ends of the wires with a small flame from a Bunsen burner. To my amazement and great satisfaction, the engine propeller started to turn slowly.

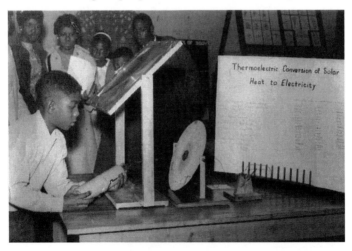

Science Fair Project

I breathed a sigh of relief, but I knew the experiment was not complete until we could demonstrate that heat from the sun, concentrated in a beam by my solar panel, would achieve the same

23

result. My dad helped with the construction of a wood frame for the solar panel. Once constructed, the panel was tilted on its base and positioned to capture the sun's rays. I'll never forget the moment when all the parts were ready for a test run. Victor and I assembled the parts on the grass in front of the school, which allowed an uninterrupted view of the sun. We focused the solar panel so that the rays from the sun began to heat the ends of the wires. After a few minutes, the propeller began to turn.

Although my compelling desire to succeed was necessary, the project was a collaborative effort, and contributions from others were essential to its success. My dad, a few of my classmates, and I had made contributions. The process of marshalling the social support to complete the project was invaluable, and I had learned an important lesson that would be with me throughout my career. Collaboration and cooperation are the ingredients for success in many endeavors.

I was ready to enter the venture in the science fair competition, which was held in an Old Tampa Fair Grounds building. We had been directed to place our projects on pre-assigned tables in a fairly large, open room the day before they were to be judged. Projects from the black schools were grouped together on the same tables. I was struck immediately by the advanced concepts from the white schools. I remember an assembled robot with wires that controlled various functions. Nevertheless, I felt that my idea was great and thought I had a chance to win recognition.

After the judging was completed, we were allowed into the room to see who had been awarded ribbons. We were disappointed that none of our entries from the black schools received a ribbon, not even an honorable mention. As we perused projects with ribbons, we identified the first, second, third and honorable mention prizes in various categories. The robot had won the overall first prize.

The next day, two of the science fair judges arrived at my high school.

"We were judges at the recently held science fair," they said, and introduced themselves to the school secretary. "We would like to meet the young fellow who submitted the solar energy entry."

I was located by the class schedule and called to the central office. As I entered, Mr. Thomas, our principal, introduced me with a big smile. "This is the student you are interested in," he said. "Ronald, I would like for you to meet these two professors from Yale University."

After an awkward moment, one of the professors spoke. "We want to apologize for not awarding you a ribbon for your project. You deserved something, but we were powerless to do anything about it." They never explained why they were powerless, but I suspect they were caught in the web of racist ideology that was a product of the times.

Later I learned that they wanted to meet my parents and to encourage me to apply to Yale after graduation. The professors never met my parents, but my mother told me, years later, "I wasn't going to send you all the way to Yale, no matter how nice those professors were."

Unbeknownst to us, Mr. Yates had entered Victor's project, two other classmates' projects, and my solar energy project in the statewide science fair competition at Florida A & M University, the all-black state university. Our spirits rose at the prospect of an opportunity to compete again and to leave home to visit a college for the first time. Mr. Yates obtained permission from our parents to drive us to Tallahassee, Florida, and the campus of Florida A & M University. Situated in a hilly area, the university was marked by red brick buildings of various sizes, separated by stretches of grass. We slept in a multistory building that housed male students. Since the competition was held during spring break, very few students were on campus. As I contemplated the college experience, I imagined the freedom from parents and teachers that college students enjoyed.

The next day we were taken to the building where the competition was held. Black high school students hoping to get the attention of the judges had traveled from various parts of the state. In the state competition, we were required to stand next to our projects while the judges questioned us. I answered technical questions about the project, my motivation for creating it, and my goals for the future. I assumed the judges were science faculty from the university, and several of them took a real interest in the project and me. That afternoon we were invited into the room for the results. I had won first prize, overall, in the competition, and Victor and the other two students won prizes in their categories. We were each awarded a ribbon and presented with a certificate. The ride home was exhilarating. We sang songs as Mr. Yates turned his car toward Tampa for the four-hour drive.

The next week a special convocation was held in the gymnasium. The Blake student body, faculty, and staff were invited. My parents were also invited. Principal Thomas presided. We were seated on the stage. He read the citations from the certificates, thanked us for representing the school, and added that everyone should be proud of our achievements.

Ronald Sheehy, Victor Buchanan, Bernard Flowers, and Ernest Boger

The audience stood in applause as our names were called. You would have thought I had hit the last-second shot in a basketball game against our cross-town rivals. In the hall, students whom I did not know came up, patted me on the back, and congratulated me.

Although I had won a science fair competition, I was an unlikely hero.

I have thought, since then, that the four of us comprised a "community of artists" even though we were in high school. In her novel *Atlas Shrugged*, Ayn Rand idealized and speculated on the possibilities of a community of artists whose works would be performed in splendid isolation from the rest of society. In her view, the corrupting values of the larger society mandated isolation for creative individuals. Her idea was extreme, of course. Very few of us have the luxury of isolation, regardless of our status or passion for our pursuits. Nevertheless, our search for personal liberation becomes more difficult because of forces in society that promote intolerance toward diversity of ideas and because of people who seemingly promote traditions and standards but actually want to preserve the status quo. Intolerant attitudes like those that produced the result in the City of Tampa Science Fair, whether prejudice, racism, or close-mindedness, must be called into question and rooted out of our society. We are fortunate in this country that overt acts of racism and prejudice have abated.

The Sit-In

— 6 —

> **Education must enable one to shift and weigh evidence, to discern the true from the false, the real from the unreal, and the facts from fiction. The function of education is to think intensively and to think critically.**
>
> **Dr. Martin Luther King Jr.**

Separate science fair competitions were one example of steps the black community took to accommodate segregation. I don't think my parents thought much about segregation in their daily activities. Only when interaction with whites was necessitated by jobs as school employees or trips downtown, where the indignities of "white only" entrances, water fountains, and bathrooms were on full display, were we reminded of our perilous and tenuous existence.

As my senior year unfolded in 1960, the civil rights movement was in full swing. Resistance to the policies of segregation across the south increased, mostly from high school and college students. Students from North Carolina A & T College staged a sit-in in Greensboro at a Woolworth's retail store on February 1, 1960. This act of defiance launched a wave of anti-segregation actions across the south.

F. W. Woolworth, Tampa

We joined the movement and held the first sit-in at a lunch counter in the Woolworth store in downtown Tampa. The event, organized by students, began with an orderly march from Blake High. Twenty seniors marched to the downtown area, which was only a fifteen-to-twenty-minute walk. Although we knew, from news reports, that other sit-ins "had been met with violence," we were not deterred. We had no training in nonviolent techniques, nor were we advised about how to respond if the event turned violent. Clearly we were stirred to undertake the protest. Fortunately no one downtown knew of our plan. We entered the store and found the lunch counter mostly deserted. With no experience, a few of us sat down at the lunch counter and waited until one of the girls broke the silence.

"We want to be served like anybody else," she said.

The lady behind the counter screamed, "Y'all betta get off those seats and get out of here, or I'm goin' to call the police."

As we sat, a crowd of shoppers and onlookers gathered behind us. I remembered the news scenes on television—students who were dragged from lunch counters or attacked as they sat on the stools.

We gathered our courage and remained seated. After a few minutes, someone started to sing the anthem of the civil rights movement, "We Shall Overcome," and we joined her. When the Tampa police arrived, I was certain we would be arrested and taken to jail, an eventuality that none of us had really considered. However, after the store manager and police conferred on a plan of action, we were advised that if we left the store, we would not be arrested. The black adult community was surprised by the event. Toward the end of our occupation of the lunch counter, Reverend Leon Lowry—head of the local NAACP Chapter, a respected voice in the black community, and pastor of one of the prominent black churches in Tampa—appeared to lend support. He attempted to mediate between the police and the students and advised us to end the protest in a dignified manner. As we dispersed, the pastor offered to drive me home, since he knew my parents. If two unrelated emotions can occupy one response, my parents were shocked and proud. A long struggle ensued, in Tampa and throughout the South, for basic human and civil rights; however, we could hardly know that, because of our courageous action that day, seeds had been planted to change race relations in Tampa.

Although our protest was courageous and heartfelt, we had no idea of the oppressive conditions that existed in our community well beyond the obvious "colored-only" water fountains and "white-only" lunch counters. The education we were provided in high school did not deal with our social reality. No analyses or discussions were offered in any of our classes to address our economic, political, and cultural predicament vis-à-vis the white majority. In fact, presentation of this type of material would have been frowned upon by school officials, and the offending teacher might have been fired.

In his book, *Pedagogy of the Oppressed*, published in 1968, Paulo Freire examined the struggle for social justice and equality by oppressed peasants in his native Brazil. Freire proposed a new approach to education that encouraged students to think critically, to ask questions, to analyze, and to inquire about the social context in which they are embedded. He criticized what he called the "banking" concept in education, in which students receive unexamined information. He also endorsed a process of dialogue between students and teachers, a process in which students are drawn to develop their own conclusions. Clearly, this approach to education would have been revolutionary during the time I was in high school during the 1950s. It is not surprising, then, that the main challenge to the system of segregation emanated from students enrolled in historically black colleges, where social issues were openly discussed and debated.

Master Teachers

To raise new questions, new possibilities, to regard old problems from a new angle, requires creative imagination and marks real advance in science.

Albert Einstein

Dr. Benjamin E. Mays

I graduated from high school in 1961, just shy of my sixteenth birthday. I applied to one college—Morehouse College—the all-male black college in Atlanta, Georgia. Morehouse was founded in 1867, two years after the Civil War had ended. Originally, the primary purpose for the school was to prepare black men for the ministry and teaching. Over the years, the college emerged at the forefront, preparing African-American males for leadership in all aspects of American life. Morehouse was also renowned for science graduates who acquired postgraduate degrees in the sciences, particularly medicine. In addition, a disproportionate number of its graduates received the PhD degree. Morehouse was the undergraduate alma mater of Dr. Martin Luther King Jr., who was the leader of the civil rights movement at the time.

Dr. Benjamin Elijah Mays, the tall, dark, stately, silver-haired president of Morehouse, had earned a national reputation as a philosopher-theologian and staunch opponent of racism and segregation in all forms. He built the college as a citadel to train black leaders with a social conscience and is regarded as the mentor to Dr. King. His autobiography, *Born to Rebel*, is a history of his personal struggle to overcome the barriers of segregation and Jim Crow practices. Dr. Mays was born to sharecropper parents in South Carolina in 1894. He beat all odds to graduate Phi Beta Kappa from Bates College and obtained the PhD degree in theology from the University of Chicago. An emphasis on intellectual competition flowed from his own desire to confront ideas of white supremacy and disprove any thought that he was inferior to anyone. According to Dr. Samuel Dubois Cook, a devoted student of Mays and President Emeritus of Dillard University, "His life was a divine romance with the world of higher possibilities."

In his autobiography, Mays writes about his quest.

> My total environment proclaimed that Negroes were inferior people, and that indictment included me. … Although I had never accepted my assigned status— or lack of it—I knew I had to prove my worth, my ability. How could I know I was not inferior to the white man, having never had a chance to compete with him? … It did not take me long to discover that Yankee superiority was as mythical as Negro inferiority.

Dr. Mays was a Christian minister who emphasized Judeo-Christian beliefs. His encouragement of academic excellence at Morehouse equaled his fervor for religious beliefs. Tuesday morning chapel was his forum for exhorting students to excel and critically examine their social situation. A former student exclaimed, "He waded into injustice unmercifully in those chapel gatherings." He expected Morehouse graduates to step up to the levels of responsibility as he had and to compete with whites on an equal basis. A natural extension of his philosophical position was the emphasis on improving the mind as a prerequisite for personal liberation. Dr. Mays set a tone and style at Morehouse that attracted the most talented African American males in the country.

Intending to give me a taste of independence, my parents put me on a train in Tampa and bade me farewell as I left for Morehouse. I think my parents gave the Pullman porter a few dollars to look out for me. Essentially, however, I was on my own. I arrived in Atlanta with much uncertainty about how I would manage to transport a fairly large trunk, as well as myself, to the college. Fortunately, enterprising upperclassmen were at the train station. After we haggled over a fee, they assisted me in the transition from the station to the college.

Graves Hall, Morehouse College

I stood in line to get my room assignment to the freshmen's dormitory, Graves Hall, and I could feel anticipation and excitement among my classmates, combined with trepidation. As I approached the "dorm mother," Mrs. Octavine Alexander, she took one look at me and sternly said, "Son, you need to tell your brother to get up here right away." She was certain that I was a stand-in for an older sibling. I could not hold this slight against her because, although I was sixteen, I am sure I looked twelve. Once I assured her that I was the enrollee, she shook her head and gave me my room assignment. Morehouse had a robust early admissions program that admitted students from the eleventh grade. A number of my classmates were only sixteen.

After a few days, I settled into the dormitory, and I made friends with Charles Ray "Sippi" (from Mississippi) Jackson, who shared my interest in tennis. We decided to play on the tennis courts behind the Atlanta University dormitories, Bumstead and Ware Hall. After the match, we stopped in Yates and Milton, a drug store on the corner of Fair and Chestnut Streets. I entered first and was asked if I were a Morehouse student by one of three tough-looking guys who stood near the door. I said, "No," and moved passed them. Charles answered, "Yes," and was immediately attacked. I turned quickly to see the melee that ensued. Charles swung his tennis racket at one of his attackers and was hit in the face by another. He fell to the floor, and all three began to stomp and kick him. One of the ladies behind the counter shouted, "I'm calling the police." Within a few moments, the three ran out of the store. My friend's face was bloody and swollen. I walked with him to the infirmary, where he was treated. Later I heard that the guys who attacked us lived in the neighborhood. We had been violently attacked because we were Morehouse students. The assault revealed the resentment and anger that some young black men who lived in the lower-income area around the college held towards Morehouse. The event marred my freshman week, which was otherwise filled with positive activities.

In 1961 Morehouse was at a crossroads, caught between the conservatism of the 1950s and the coming revolution of the 1960s. During the fall of my freshmen year, fellow students launched a "panty raid" on Spelman College, the all-girls college across the street. Within that same month, students organized a sit-in at a downtown lunch counter in Atlanta. I don't think it occurred to us how our involvement in both these activities was contradictory. Yet the high jinks of the 1950s, the panty raids and such, would make way for more serious actions that confronted segregation and Jim Crow.

My best friend, Allen Carter, and I decided to participate in a planned sit-in at Grady Hospital, the segregated public hospital in downtown Atlanta. When we arrived, the police had cordoned off the area in the lobby of the hospital. Officers directed students who were willing to go to jail to a specific area. The rest were told to leave the building. I was informed at the time that if I went to jail as a minor, I would be deported from the state. With no knowledge of the law, I left the building. Allen decided to join the group that was going to jail and ended up in the county jail. A few days later, Allen and the students were bailed out, and returned to campus triumphantly dressed in county jail uniforms.

Atlanta was home to the offices of the Student Non-violent Coordinating Committee (SNCC), and Morehouse students were leaders and officers in that organization. As the 1960s unfolded, Atlanta played a pivotal role in the civil rights movement as the home base for Dr. King's organization, the Southern Christian Leadership Council (SCLC).

The most challenging course for all science majors during the freshmen year was general chemistry, taught by the feared Dr. Henry Cecil McBay. His course was the prerequisite for the other science courses. For those who flunked the first semester, no trailer course was available. Those who failed usually changed majors and chose some field other than the sciences. Dr. McBay is credited with increasing the ranks of preachers and political scientists, a number of whom became very accomplished and famous.

I performed well on the first test, scoring in the nineties; however, I scored in the forties on the second test. I needed a respectable score on the final in order to pass the course. The night before the final, I visited the small chapel on campus to ask God to intervene on my behalf. The next morning, I was startled to see Dr. McBay walking briskly toward the chemistry building.

I thought, "What sort of omen is this?" General chemistry was a high stakes course, and everyone on campus was curious to know who had passed and who had failed. Dr. McBay's ritual was to communicate this news during registration for the second semester of the course. We lined up single file, and as we approached the distinguished professor, he consulted his roll book and indicated whether each student had passed or failed.

Fortunately, I passed. In my class, however, we had an 80 percent attrition rate. The lecture room, which was filled during the first semester, was pretty sparsely populated with the remaining 20 percent as we began the second semester. One might question the educational rationale for such high attrition rates. Clearly, under a different approach, more capable students could have continued as science majors. However, the winnowing process ensured that Morehouse would produce an incomparable cadre of highly capable science undergraduates. The course contributed to the Morehouse reputation as an institution with high standards. Dr. McBay's legacy is his graduation of more black students who attained the PhD in chemistry than any other individual in the country.

The fraternity system was a major feature of student life at Morehouse. Throughout the period of segregation and Jim Crow, black fraternities and sororities became a powerful social force within the black community, as well as on black campuses.

I pledged Alpha Phi Alpha Fraternity, founded in 1906, the oldest of the black fraternities. During the pledge period, we were forced-marched to Ebenezer Church, a forty-minute walk from campus, to hear Dr. Martin Luther King Jr., "an Alpha man." On occasion Dr. King would schedule time in his civil rights activities to return home to preach at his church in Atlanta. That Sunday he delivered an inspiring sermon on the civil rights movement, "Epitaph and Challenge." The discourse illuminated the religious and spiritual foundations related to the struggle for freedom in the nation. After the sermon, we lined up single-file to meet Dr. King, who greeted us individually and shook our hands. We lined up shortest to tallest, which placed me at the front of the line.

As I approached, he extended his hand and said, "Well, when I was at Morehouse, I thought I was short, but, son, you might have me beat. How about the Spelman girls, are they treating you all right?" I didn't know whether he was joking or not. And even though he was the civil rights leader, at the time, I didn't appreciate the joke. Of course, as I recall the incident, I was very proud to meet Dr. King. I have remembered the rather humorous comment about height and girls, with great pride, as my special connection to Dr. King.

Although I felt I had adapted to the social and academic aspects of college life, I was not particularly motivated. My grades were average, and the spark that I felt in high school—the interest in astronomy, the science fair competition—had slowly receded in my consciousness. Something was missing.

Dr. Roy Hunter Jr., recently hired assistant professor of biology, worked in an office on the first floor of John Hope Hall, the location of the biology department. His glasses rode very low on a broad nose and barely extended to his ears. A relatively short man, he looked like a wrestler from the waist up. I saw him on occasion as he moved up and down steps and through the halls on crutches. I learned that he suffered from polio and had been dealing with mobility issues since childhood.

Dr. Roy Hunter, Jr.

Dr. Hunter was a Morehouse graduate, class of 1953, and later graduated with the PhD in Developmental Biology from Brown University. His was no small achievement, and not only because of his physical challenges. When he graduated from Morehouse, the majority of graduate schools in the country were closed to blacks. Trained as a research scientist, Dr. Hunter returned to Morehouse with a consummate desire to make a difference in the lives of students and with a focus on experimental embryology. We were intrigued with the new professor, and a number of us enrolled in the embryology course he was slated to teach that semester. The first day of class, Dr. Hunter discussed the textbook. "Gentlemen, the text I have chosen will describe the latest experimental approaches employed to understand the differentiation of cells. Many of the articles will not provide answers, but will leave you with profound questions about the nature of cells."

I could not believe what I had heard. Something in my mind was turned on like a light in a dark room. The ideas of unanswered questions and new experimental approaches caught my attention. I had felt the same way about science in high school; now someone had rekindled my desire to examine so-called facts and to ask questions. The professor's lectures were infused with "what if" questions and analysis and evaluation of cutting-edge research. In an age before the widespread use of overhead projectors and PowerPoint presentations, Dr. Hunter had mastered the use of the blackboard. His lectures were painstakingly planned and illustrated. He used different colors of chalk to illustrate various tissue types in beautifully crafted drawings on the board as he supported himself on two crutches. I was so motivated by his teaching style and presentations that I could not wait for the next class. The first exam, a take-home exam, was memorable. We could take the exam to our rooms, answer the questions, and return it at a required time the next day. In each question, a problem from the journal articles was posed. He asked us to discuss the nature of the problem and provide an analysis of the results. The approach, of course, required us to integrate information from a variety of sources into a narrative that followed logically from our research of the topic. Dr. Hunter didn't care whether we discussed the questions with each other or not, since each student's response depended on his own preparation and perspective. The first exam consisted of three questions, and I remember turning in twenty pages. He read every word and wrote comments in the margins. Throughout the semester, he managed to grade all papers and return them, with comments, in a timely fashion. I continued to write page after page in response to his exam questions. In fact, he teased, "Mr. Sheehy, I think you have contracted some kind of virus that produces a diarrhea of thought on paper."

I wondered if he knew the effect he had, not just on me but on the entire class. He taught us how to ask questions and implored us to use our intellectual talents to evaluate methods and results of scientific experiments. He was teaching us to think critically. Most of all, he respected our opinions and insisted that they be supported by sound analysis and reasoning.

The Civil Rights Movement was a cry for freedom, social justice, and civil rights, Dr. Hunter taught a different kind of liberty—the freedom of inquiry. He was, by far, the best teacher I have ever experienced. He wanted us to appreciate and fully understand the nature of science. He knew that challenging assumptions and rigorously examining supposed facts could lead to new insights and progress in science. I had found a mentor and kindred spirit.

Restaurants

— **8** —————————————————————————————

On July 2, 1964, the Civil Rights Act of 1964 was passed. The act outlawed racial segregation in schools, public places, and employment. The momentous event occurred between my junior and senior year, when I was home for the summer. The Act, signed by President Lyndon Johnson with Dr. King directly behind him, was broadcast on national television. While the Act outlawed discrimination in schools and employment, the elimination of discrimination in public places—or public accommodations—was immediate and dramatic. As I watched the proceedings with my mother, I wondered, "What is she thinking?" Her generation had accommodated segregation in all of its aspects. Her age group had carved out, as much as possible, a separate social existence from whites.

"Well, I guess we can now get a hot dog at the lunch counter that you and your friends picketed during your high school year," she said sarcastically. I thought she would be overjoyed, but I detected more of a "wait and see" attitude. Weeks later, I proposed to my parents that we try out the "public accommodations" aspects of the new law and visit a previously segregated restaurant in Tampa. I didn't know how they would react to the suggestion; they consented to give it a try after a little coaxing. We chose a restaurant on Dale Mabry Highway, only a short drive from our house in West Tampa. My dad and mother dressed up in their Sunday best. Dad wore a dark pinstripe suit, white shirt, and tie. He looked very much the school principal. My mother wore a dark dress with a string of pearls around her neck. The day was hot, so I decided not to wear a coat, but I did wear a shirt and tie. The ride to the restaurant was short; however, it seemed a hundred miles away. We had no conversation about strategy, what to do if we were not served—or, worse, if we were attacked physically. I was frightened, not for myself, but for my response if my parents were embarrassed by hostile words or acts.

My mother sought to assure my dad that everything would be all right. "Now, Val, I don't want you to say a word. If anything is said to you, I will respond, do you understand?" she said, with the conviction that she knew best.

I followed them into the restaurant. As we opened the glass doors, I noticed that the room was set up in cafeteria style, and our first act was to get trays and move into the line behind other patrons. The young lady in charge gave us a faint smile and, without saying a word, greeted us and urged us on. I tried not to look around, but I could not avoid the stares and grimacing faces of the seated whites as we moved through the line. We selected our food, received a receipt, walked toward an empty table, and sat down. Conversation between us was minimal, and we managed to eat a full meal without much talk. The tension, which was evident as we entered, had evaporated somewhat, and we relaxed. People stopped staring, and the rest of our visit was without incident. I suspect that my parents summoned considerable courage to confront an unpleasant situation that they had lived with for their entire lives. Think of it—at some point, every restaurant or public accommodation, which had previously been segregated, was visited just once by black people and then became desegregated. No standing ovations or plaques were presented for these acts of courage.

When I returned to Morehouse in September, I was anxious to repeat the experience of personal participation in desegregation, and I recruited a friend to join me in desegregating a restaurant on Peachtree Street. We recruited two young ladies from Spelman to accompany us. Dressed in our Sunday best, we drove to an upscale restaurant near the train station on Peachtree Street. As we drove to the restaurant, we felt none of the fear or concern that had accompanied my parents. We were ready to exercise our rights and were looking good to boot. My buddy, Lovell Mosely of California, offered to drive. He did not fully appreciate the significance of our sojourn.

He kept saying, "Why is it such a big deal? I've been eating around whites all my life."

"How is that?" one of our dates joked. "The only food blacks can get in a white restaurant in California is takeout."

We pulled into the parking lot of the restaurant in good spirits. The maitre d' greeted us with a big smile. "How many in your party?"

"Four, please," I said confidently. We were led to a table outfitted with white linen and decorative flowers. The clientele, who were clearly older and, from their attire, pretty well-heeled, seemed to give us little notice.

Within a few minutes, our waitress arrived, "My name is Alice, and I'll be serving y'all today," she said with a bubbly exuberance. As she handed us menus, she said, "I am so excited! I have never served Negroes before."

The rejoinder to that line is, "And we have never eaten any Negroes," but she seemed genuinely enthused, so we ignored her comment.

From that point on, she fussed over us like a mother hen. "Was the food all right? Did we need more water? Where were we from?" Eventually she volunteered information that she wanted to go to college and told us we were lucky to be in college. She said she would never forget this day and that she was going to tell her friends that she was the first in the restaurant to serve Negroes.

Biases and intolerances in our social relations, whether of ethnic, gender-based, or religious origin, affect both individual and societal development in a profound way. The small and large slights that segregation engendered were vexations to the human spirit, and made social relations between white and black Americans torturous and awkward even after desegregation. It is seldom acknowledged that segregation affected the creative potential of both blacks and whites. Both were caught in a web of laws and customs, which inhibited free expression in individuals from all fields of endeavor and robbed our society of enormous individual potential.

Letter from Dad

— 9 —

I was filled with uncertainty throughout 1965, my senior year at Morehouse. We were fearful of the possibility of being drafted for the Vietnam War. A number of my classmates considered going to Canada to avoid the draft. I worried constantly about whether I would amass the credits required to graduate. At the top of my worry list was, "How would I pass German?" Dr. Rose Marie Akselrad, originally from Germany, had taught German at Morehouse for more than a decade. Her strict grading standards fed my anxiety.

In her halting German accent, Dr. Akselrad said, "Mr. Sheehy, I understand you do well in science, so I don't understand why you can't do well in German. If you don't pull up your grade, I give you F!"

She offered no idle threats. I knew that if I received an F in her class, I would not graduate on time. As college seniors have done for years, I had already affirmed to my parents that I would graduate in May.

The complexities of figuring out my future after graduation also weighed heavily on my mind. In addition, I was dating at the time and recognized my need for advice about relationships with the opposite sex. I turned to Dad and asked him to write to me about "love and relationships."

I am sure my request struck him as an odd one. However, he said, "Let me give this some thought."

On an overcast day, I made the routine trek to the post office on campus. The postmistress was Mrs. Flora Collins Lamar, a buxom woman, a fixture at the college. She lived in an apartment in the freshmen's dormitory and belonged to a cadre of women who dedicated themselves to Morehouse students as surrogate mothers.

A long line of students impatiently waited in front of the post office for Mrs. Lamar to open the window. As each student approached, she often said, with a smile that could melt butter, "Nothing today." Most times we did not need to tell our names. Her familiarity, at times, was most disconcerting since we often wondered if she had overlooked a special letter or package from home.

On this particular overcast day, I expected the smile and familiar refrain, "Nothing today." I was surprised when she said, "Mr. Sheehy, you have a letter."

I immediately recognized, from the handwriting on the envelope, that the letter was from Dad. As I walked back to my dorm, I began to read.

> Dear Ronald,
>
> I hope this letter finds you in good spirits and health. The last time we talked, you asked me to provide thoughts about "love and relationships." I have not, in many years, given much thought to the idea of love. Perhaps, in our busy lives, we ignore our need for love. Or, we take love for granted. My mother always reminded me that in order to receive (genuine) love, we have to give love in return. I have not always lived up to that standard. I hope you will consider this as good advice.

Love is often used as a noun, as in the lyric, "Love is a many splendored thing." A sunset, a beautiful art object, or a masterfully created piece of music, are objects of love. While we feel passion and affection for these things, it is not the same as the commitment, which should define the love between a man and woman, or between God and his creation.

The love that flows between a man and woman requires understanding, patience, and most of all forgiveness. Understanding is required in order to see through the mask that most of us wear everyday, which obscures motives underlying good and bad actions. Patience is required so that we withhold judgment until we have comprehended all of the facts. And finally, we have to forgive so we can release ourselves and others from the chains of resentment, vindictiveness and reprisal. If these aspects of love are practiced, you will have a healthy relationship, and the commitment to love each other will be easy to attain. In their absence, hatred, resentment, envy and anger are the inevitable consequences and the commitment to love will be difficult.

You know, I am not a church-going man, and I hope you didn't misinterpret this as a disinterest in spirituality. I think the life force that flows through creation, is another way of interpreting or defining God. I believe, God, provides in every way for his creation, and in return, we should "love God with all our soul and heart." When we feel separate from this divine love, through our focus on selfishness and ego, we are like a branch cut from a tree, which eventually will wither and die.

I encourage you to remain open for love in all its manifestations, and to find a measure of love in your work. Search for that special mate, as I have found with your mother, who you can love without reservation and enjoy for a lifetime.

Sincerely,

Dad

I mentioned Dad's letter to my roommate, Ruben Brigety, who became the first black medical student accepted at the University of Florida. I told him that my dad had written a letter that I thought was quite profound. He read it and described the letter to one of his friends. Eventually my special note was passed around throughout the dorm. Guys would periodically stop by my room to ask, "Who has the letter?"

I passed German and received approval from the registrar's office to graduate in May.

Graduation

— 10 —

A Morehouse tradition—ended for reasons that will be clarified presently—was a dance-till-dawn on the eve of graduation day. Sponsored by the Kappas, the Kappa Dawn Dance was held in an event facility (dance hall) not far from campus. Graduation practice was led by Dean Bradford Brazille, a gentleman of the old school, who frequently reminded us of proper etiquette.

He instructed us to take two handkerchiefs when out on dates. "Use one to blow your nose, and the other to hand to the young lady." We sat in rapt attention as he warned us of the perils of the Kappa Dawn Dance.

"Gentlemen, we are not going to have you excusing yourself during the ceremony because you can't hold your liquor. Last year we had a soon-to-be Morehouse man run down the aisle during the President's charge to the class. We are going to have none of that, this year. Is that understood?" he said emphatically.

We got that, but we listened to a different call—the anticipation of a well-deserved good time.

We stumbled out of the dance around six AM with only two hours until the graduation ceremonies began promptly at eight AM. Parents who had no idea of the revelry of the prior night would have been uniformly upset at a no-show. I managed to get to my room, dress, and get in line just before eight AM. My head was spinning as we marched in, and I made every effort to keep my eyes open. I couldn't wait to get the pomp and circumstances finished and return to my room for some needed sleep.

Through the fog in my consciousness, I heard the voice of President Mays. He had risen to give the charge to the class. I had heard him many times, but the solemnity of his tone grabbed my attention.

> Never again will I speak to all of you together. Time and fate will see to that. So I dare not lose this opportunity to bequeath to you my parting words. They will probably do no good; but like the prophets of Israel, I must have my say.
>
> I do not know what impression you have of Morehouse; but whatever it is, during these four years, you have helped to make it better or worse. You are part and parcel of Morehouse. You have helped to weave the fabric out of which this institution is made.
>
> It may not be the best college in the world, but we have high ideals and some of us love it. We shall try to implement these ideals. Even when we fail, we shall never cease to try, for low aim and low ideals, not failure, are the deadly sins.
>
> For ninety-eight years this institution has striven to make men free and responsible. Born and nurtured in a segregated economy which cramps the mind, stifles the soul, and circumscribes the heart, Morehouse has always taught that the mind can be free in a tightly segregated society; that a man's body could ride, sleep, eat, worship, and work in a segregated society without ever being segregated. Our philosophy has been, and is now, that no man is a slave, no man is in prison, and no man is segregated

until he accepts it in his mind. The minds of Paul, John Bunyan, Nehru, Fred Douglass, and Martin Luther King Jr. were never in bondage. For ninety-eight years this has been our philosophy. But we face now a crucial hour in our history. We could miss the meaning of desegregation and integration.

You are the most fortunate class that has ever graduated from Morehouse. Barriers of segregation are falling so fast that they make the timid and the insecure dizzy. Desegregation and integration will not of themselves make men free. It is highly conceivable that one can live and work and have his being in a desegregated society, cringing and cow-towing at the same time. Desegregation and integration are not ends but means.

Certainly, the end of segregation in church and school, in train and plane, on land and sea, in hotel and motel, in employment and recreation, is not merely to be with other Americans. It is not to give one a false notion of his worth, to make him believe that he has arrived—that he has risen higher in the world, that he is automatically more important as a person because he can eat in the finest restaurant, sleep in the swankiest hotel, work side by side with any American and socialize freely. These are not the ends of a desegregated society. Americans disguised as Communists, intent on overthrowing the United States Government, Nazis spreading the poison of hate, the members of the Ku Klux Klan, the wealthy who make their millions in the underworld of prostitution, alcoholism, and dope can and do enjoy these luxuries unsegregated and without embarrassment.

To state the case more positively, the end of segregation and eventually integration, should be to unshackle the minds of Negro youth, loose the chain from the Negro's soul, free his heart from fear and intimidation so that he will be able to develop whatever gifts God has given him, and share the fruits of his mind and soul with humanity around the globe in the arts and sciences, in the professions and sports, in business and industry, in medicine and law, in music and dance, and in painting and sculpture.

Dr. Mays made a case for a freedom beyond the dimensions of civil rights that included the freedom of mind, the freedom to create, the freedom of opinion and expression, and the freedom to inquire, as Dr. Hunter had emphasized. He clearly saw beyond the superficial benefits of integration and encouraged us to seek liberties of the mind as the ultimate freedom.

His words rattled around in my consciousness, and years passed before their impact manifested in my own life. Dr. Mays concluded the speech with a passion for us to feel the weight of his specific challenge.

We want Morehouse men to enter a desegregated society standing erect on their feet, accepting all the rights, privileges and responsibilities inherent in a free society. And wherever you go, Atlanta, Chicago, Harvard, or Yale; whatever you do, whatever you say, never forget that you are a Morehouse Man, and that the College will never release you from the obligation to strive to do whatever you do so well that no man living, no man dead and no man yet to be born could do the work any better than you.

To this day, I am inspired by his words. Could the bar have been set any higher? Dr. Mays planted seeds for a true revolution of the mind and the spirit. Dr. Martin Luther King Jr. had accepted the torch and proclaimed that Dr. Mays was his "intellectual and spiritual mentor." King added, "He has been a source of hope for the hopeless, a strong motivator for the unmotivated, and a shining light

Martin Luther King, Jr. and Benjamin E. Mays

of inspiration for those who have walked through the darkness of oppression." Mays and King were leaders who had the courage of their convictions and inspired the support of an ever-widening circle of supporters to the cause of equality and justice.

At the end of the graduation service, we sang the college hymn, "Dear Old Morehouse," a melodious, soul-stirring song, written by J. O. B. Mosely, class of 1929. I was now a Morehouse Man. Howard Thurman (1899–1981), a Morehouse graduate who is thought to be one of the greatest theologians of the twentieth century, made clear the responsibility of a Morehouse graduate. He intoned, "They placed over our heads a crown that for the rest of our lives we would be trying to grow tall enough to wear."

I have often thought of my undergraduate years and the most significant lessons of the period. I think one of the most important challenges for the teenage years, whether one attends college or not, is not to be defined by failure and to keep a drive for success in perspective. To paraphrase Rudyard Kipling, "Success and failure are both imposters, treat them both the same." Along the highway of life, often the measure of success or failure is arbitrary. I am also reminded of the importance of the friendships established during my college days. Lasting relationships provide support through the changing tide of circumstance that is the inevitable consequence of life.

The Employment Test

I stayed in Atlanta after graduation in hopes of landing a job. Three weeks passed with no luck, and I was running out of money. Often, when I needed help in the past, I had called on an old friend of my dad, Mr. Julius "Skip" Lockett, the Business Officer at Morehouse. Mr. Lockett was a short, barrel-chested man with a crooked smile. He and my dad were teammates on the Bethune Cookman College football team in the 1930s. I opened the door to his office, and I noticed that his secretary had stepped away from her desk. Her absence was my good fortune. Getting past his secretary was like trying to get into Fort Knox.

"Hello, Mr. Lockett," I said.

He looked up from his work. "Well, congratulations on your graduation. I knew you could do it, and I know your dad is proud that you are not on the five- or six-year plan. "

"Thank you," I said, and got right to the point of my visit. "Mr. Lockett, I need a job for the summer, otherwise I'm going to have to return to Tampa."

"Son, I haven't seen you in months," he said, a bit irritated. "How's your dad?"

"He's fine," I said.

"Did he come for graduation?" he asked.

"Of course," I said.

"Well, he didn't look me up," as if to say, *You and your dad only see me when you need something.*

"Aw, Mr. Lockett, it's not like that. You know how it is during graduation with trying to manage parents and relatives. It does not leave a lot of time to visit."

He appeared to accept my point and relaxed a little. "Well, I got a call the other day from an employment agency looking to hire a few college graduates for the summer. Here's the address downtown. You should call immediately for an appointment." He paused, and his tone turned serious. "You know, Ronald, the Civil Rights Act passed last year, and it prohibits discrimination in employment. Opportunities like this are going to be open for you young people."

The next day I called for an appointment with the employment agency. A gentleman answered the phone. I inquired about a job opening. He hesitated until I mentioned that Mr. Lockett at Morehouse had referred me. The man's tone changed, and he set an appointment for 9:00 AM the next day.

Unwilling to be late, I arrived at 8:30 AM. The directory in the foyer indicated that the agency was on the fifth floor. I took the elevator and then knocked on the door of the Wilson Employment Agency. A voice behind the door told me to come in. Seated at a desk was an elderly white gentleman. I reached out my hand to shake his hand.

As our hands clasped, he said, "I'm Mr. Wilson, and I own this agency."

"Pleased to meet you," I said.

"I understand that you are here about the stock assistant job," he said, peering at me over his glasses.

"That's right, Mr. Wilson, Mr. Lockett at Morehouse told me about this opportunity."

"Okay. Why don't you fill out this application, and we'll get you started," he said.

The application was short, and I returned it to him after about ten minutes.

"I see you are a college graduate," he said without looking up. "I am sure, then, you are not going to have a problem with this little employment test. It will take you about thirty minutes. Why don't you step into this vacant room across the hall, and you can get started."

The test was multiple-choice. Several questions required my interpretation of a passage, and another section contained simple math problems. As I plowed through the test, I wondered why this prerequisite to obtain a minimum wage position as a "stock boy." *Never mind*, I said to myself, *just do your best*. I finished and returned the test to Mr. Wilson.

"Have a seat," he said. "It won't take long to get your score."

As he corrected my answers, he uttered peculiar sounds. I tried not to pay attention. Finally he finished and tabulated my score, and then he looked at me, appearing bemused.

"You know, young man, the test you took will let us know if you have the ability to perform the task assigned to you," he said in a stern voice. "The employer requires that we give all prospective employees this test, and a minimum score is required. I'm sorry, but you did not reach the minimum score, and I can't offer you the job."

I didn't linger. I thanked him and left immediately. As I emerged from the building, I felt dizzy from the experience. I was devastated. Conflicting emotions battered my mind. First, I was embarrassed that I did not perform to represent my ability, or so he said. Second, I knew that I possessed the ability and background to do the job, so why was I judged by a test so unrelated to the job? Yet, I reasoned, the company had to utilize a process to screen out incompetent applicants. Or was the exam a ruse to present an appearance of fairness? I wrestled with my ambivalence and vowed that in the future, I would not let a test of any sort stand between me and my goals.

Today, young people need to be made aware of the importance of standardized testing to their future. Whether one wants to be a fireman, teacher, lawyer or doctor, he or she must do well on standardized test. As educators and parents, we need to do a better job of preparing students for the world of standardized testing. The problem does not start with the test, but with preparation in test taking skills and in the command of content areas, particularly math and reading.

Atlanta University

12

The irony of my experience with Mr. Wilson and his employment test was apparent when I received a notice from Atlanta University later in the summer. The letter reflected the score that I received on the Graduate Record Exam (GRE), and stated that I had been accepted into the Master Program in Biology at Atlanta University.

Atlanta University was established in 1897, following the Civil War, to train teachers for the children of approximately one-half million illiterate former slaves. In order to accomplish this goal, a "normal" (or, primary) school was established initially, which led to the development of a high school and an undergraduate college. Around 1929, President John Hope developed a plan to create graduate programs, and a formal university structure was established in 1930. In his seminal work, *The Story of Atlanta University,* historian Dr. Clarence Bacote writes that, by the end of the 1930s and the early 1940s, "The University had become a regional institution, admitting more Negro students as candidates for advanced degrees, and awarded more such degrees than any other institution in the nation." By 1950, one-third of all blacks who earned master's degrees in American universities were graduated from Atlanta University. The only historically black institution devoted exclusively to graduate education, the university attracted a distinguished faculty during its storied history. None was more distinguished than Dr. W. E. B. Du Bois, who is regarded as one of the greatest intellectuals of his day. Atlanta University merged with Clark College in 1988 and is now Clark Atlanta University.

In 1932 Dr. Samuel Nabrit, a 1925 Morehouse graduate, was the first black to receive a PhD degree from Brown University. He was an accomplished marine biologist and became chair of the Department of Biology at Atlanta University. During his time at Atlanta University, he influenced a promising student, Roy Hunter Jr., to become a biologist and follow his path at Brown University. We are often unaware of the lineage of influences in our lives. It is clear to me that Dr. Nabrit's love of research and biology influenced Dr. Hunter, who later passed that enthusiasm on to me.

Throughout my undergraduate years, I was aware of the biology department at Atlanta University. The department was located in a highly visible two-story white stucco building only yards from Hope Hall, the Morehouse biology building. One of the prominent features of the building was the glass-enclosed seminar room, and in the evening, I watched students and faculty dressed in white coats as they assembled for a seminar.

The Department of Biology had amassed a distinguished faculty who held PhD degrees from the finest Northern universities. The faculty was led by Dr. Lafayette Frederick, a botanist—and a giant of a man, both physically and intellectually. I was excited about the challenge and took advanced courses in biology. I reunited with Dr. Hunter, who transferred to Atlanta University my senior year at Morehouse. The first semester, I signed up for courses with Dr. Hunter and Dr. Frederick. I knew what to expect from Dr. Hunter and got large doses of his teaching style with the take-home exams. I was surprised how demanding Dr. Frederick was. Dr. Hunter was concerned with ideas; Dr. Frederick was equally concerned with details. Dr. Frederick required us to know the names of hundreds of fungi, both the genus and species name, and to be able to identify them by sight. In both classes, a good-natured competition for the highest grade was waged, especially among Morehouse graduates.

Toward the end of the second semester, I asked Dr. Hunter to serve as my thesis advisor, and he consented. We decided on a project that involved an investigation of the effects of beryllium nitrate on the regeneration of tail tissue in tadpole (*Rana pipens*) larvae. Beryllium nitrate is widely used in nuclear reactors, space devices, electronics, and other specialized purposes. Therefore, the toxicology of the chemical to living systems, particularly humans, was of considerable interest. My project was to expose tadpoles to various concentrations of beryllium nitrate, amputate the tails, and look—both histologically and histochemically—at the regenerative tissue for damage. I concluded that beryllium nitrate, at certain concentrations, affects tail regeneration in tadpole larvae; also, more specifically, that it affects the synthesis of cellular building blocks. These results raised more questions than I could answer, especially at the biochemical level. I had begun to understand that the search for answers in science is, in many instances, inconclusive, and this uncertainty drives exploration and expands possibilities. While I enjoyed the speculation of underlying mechanisms, I knew I had barely scratched the surface in regard to an understanding of the causes and effects involved. The next step for me had to be a PhD in the biological sciences.

While arriving at this decision, I experienced some good fortune. I finished work toward the master's degree and decided to get married during the same time period. Pat Blanco and I had dated during the previous two years. She was from Tampa and attended Fisk University in Nashville, Tennessee. Our plan was to return to Tampa and move in with my parents. We would both enroll in the University of South Florida in Tampa. She would finish her undergraduate studies, and I would enroll in the PhD program. We were hopeful about the future.

University of South Florida

13

In 1967 the Vietnam War was raging, and the country was caught in the throes of the civil rights movement—it was a tumultuous time. I was married to my new bride. As planned, we moved back to Tampa and into my parents' house. I was back in my old room, but this time sharing it with someone else. Before I left Atlanta, I had applied to the program in biology in the graduate school at the University of South Florida in Tampa. During the summer I received an acceptance letter, including a tuition grant and a stipend so that I could matriculate in September. The University of South Florida, similar to other institutions in the South, had been integrated for only a few years. In 1961 my high school classmate, Ernest Boger, had been the first black to enroll in the university as an undergraduate.

Located north of Tampa, the university was an emerging campus, established as a major university in 1956. Its relatively few buildings were separated by long stretches of grass and connected with sidewalks. Built in an open style that is typical in South Florida schools, the offices and laboratories, particularly the biology building, opened into corridors that were open to the outside. The architecture created a very "laid back" campus. Most of the time, shorts and sandals were the preferred dress. Although I thought I was prepared, I was uncertain whether I could compete with white students. Morehouse had impressed upon me that, as a "Morehouse Man," I was duty-bound to perform in a way that was beyond reproach. The words of President Mays, in his charge to the seniors only two years before, still rang in my ears. He had intoned, "Let no man say he could do a job better than a Morehouse Man." Morehouse did a good job of inspiring its graduates to have high expectations.

The roster of successful Morehouse men, a testament to the tradition, offered me no solace. I had my own cross to bear. Sure, I had grown up in close proximity to whites, yet my community and theirs had little or no contact. Segregation had robbed us of the opportunity to know one another. The assumptions of inferiority weighed heavily on my mind. The thought that I would be judged as less than capable was unsettling. On my first day at the university, I felt great apprehension. Would I be insulted? Would questions be asked of me that I could not answer? Would I represent "the race" appropriately? Thoughts darted across my mind as I drove toward the University for the first meeting.

I parked in a sparsely populated parking lot and walked down a long sidewalk toward the biology building. I entered the office of the chairman, Dr. Robert Long, and was greeted warmly by the secretary. After a short time, a dignified white gentlemen, not much taller than I, emerged from the back office and shook my hand firmly. Some whites had an aversion to physical contact with blacks; therefore, a limp handshake or a quick release was a tip-off to a prejudiced attitude. I detected none of that from Dr. Long.

I think he sensed my apprehension. He said unhesitatingly, "We are pleased you chose USF. When I first saw your application, I was anxious to meet you."

He referred to the excellent recommendation I received from Dr. Frederick, the department chair at Atlanta University. He said he knew Dr. Frederick, since they were both botanists, and had immense respect for his contribution to the field. The statement of familiarity relaxed me immediately, and we had a congenial conversation. He wanted to know my interest so that he could introduce me to an advisor and develop an appropriate course sequence. He admitted that the department was relatively new. Moreover, the PhD program had been recently inaugurated. I didn't want to make a hasty decision, so I postponed the selection of an advisor until I could determine my interest and orient myself with professors in the department. During the conversation, I learned that I would not be placed in the PhD program automatically; I would be required to complete a master's degree program first. Since I already held a master's degree, that requirement did not sit well with me.

However, that day was not the time for protest. I was required by law to register with my Selective Service board. If I remained out of school, I would have surely been drafted. Various levels of deferments were available. Enrollment in a college or university provided a reason to defer, and if one were married, with children, he would be even lower on the list to be selected. I met two of the criteria; I was married and in school.

Dr. John V. Betz

Although I took a number of courses that first semester, microbial genetics, taught by Dr. John Betz, was most interesting. Dr. Betz was a bit of a maverick. He chain-smoked and bounced around the building as if only he knew the revealed secrets of microbial biochemistry and the new field of molecular biology. He had received his PhD degree in virology from St. Bonaventure at a time when new concepts and theories in biology were emerging. Armed with a brilliant mind for analysis and a great memory of biochemical pathways, Dr. Betz introduced me to the paradigm shift in biology that followed the discovery of the functions of DNA. His matter-of-fact teaching style, unlike Dr. Hunter's questioning approach, was casual but direct. He reveled in the ability to describe recent progress in biology with precision and in excruciating detail. I was enthralled with the new research findings in biology that fell under the general heading of molecular biology and with the cleverness of the experimental approaches.

At the end of Dr. Betz's class, I was ready to select my thesis advisor and plan the direction of my studies. Since I had done well in his class, Dr. Betz consented to be my advisor. On the whole, I found the other graduate students to be congenial and, on occasion, helpful. My office mate, with whom I related well, was not married. Unfortunately, perhaps since he was single, he was drafted during the second semester. Very few black undergraduates attended USF. I don't think I met another black graduate student the first year, although a few might have studied in other fields. The racial environment near the campus was mixed. Blacks could frequent various hippie hangouts without problems, but there was no guarantee that they would be served in nearby restaurants without incident. If I wanted to eat at a restaurant near campus, I never went alone, but always with a group of fellow students.

On April 4, 1968, Dr. Martin Luther King Jr. was assassinated. I was on campus when the news bulletin was broadcast. I remember feeling disoriented. I walked the halls aimlessly, avoiding conversation.

I ran into Dr. Betz in the hallway, and he said, "Ron, why don't you go home?"

"I might consider that," I said.

As I continued to walk, various students and a number of faculty members expressed regret and offered words of sympathy for what they knew to be a tremendous loss for black Americans. I left campus early and drove home in a daze.

Following the assassination, the black community across the country exploded in rage. Tampa was not spared from the wrath, which manifested through incidents of burning and looting in the black community that continued for days.

On the second day of the rioting in Tampa, my Morehouse friend, Dr. Benjamin Berry, and I attempted to quell some of the violence. Ben had come to Tampa, fresh from the Harvard Divinity School, to work in the inner city and to establish a ministry for the United Church of Christ. I became interested in Ben's youth program and was allowed to organize evening programs at a community center designed to discuss the black dilemma, as well as black history. We thought that, by virtue of our work with youth in the area, we had earned a measure of credibility with some of the neighborhood toughs who were engaged in the violence.

A neighborhood bar on Twenty-Second Street was a hangout for young men who, as the sun went down, engaged in burning and looting in the black neighborhoods. Our goal was to help them to see the damage to their own community as they blindly raged against those presumed responsible for the murder of Dr. King.

Confident in our good intentions, Ben and I walked into the bar. We approached a group of rather hard-looking guys who sat around a table.

Ben spoke to the young men. "I'm Reverend Berry, and I live a couple of blocks over from here. I'm concerned that what Dr. King stood for—a non-violent approach—is being destroyed by senseless destruction."

One of the fellows stood up and pointed at us. "Who the hell do you think you are, coming up in here lecturing to us?" He waved his hands in the air.

"I am a minister, young man, and it is my duty to bear witness when I see wrong," Ben said.

Another spoke up, "Oh, so you supposed to be Dr. King's replacement, huh? I think you better get out of here and take your sidekick with you." I felt that our approach was a hopeless cause, no matter how well-intentioned. I pulled on Ben's sleeve and motioned him to move backward and out the door. We had just seen, up close, the anger that has been called *black rage*. If we had not left when we did, that rage could have turned on us.

On April 9, 1968, five days after the assassination, thousands of people gathered on the campus of Morehouse College for funeral services for Dr. King. Millions more watched the proceedings on television, as did my mother and I. The speaker's podium was set on the portico of Harkness Hall, the Atlanta University administration building. The building faced an open, grassy area that extended about two hundred yards north to Graves Hall, the Morehouse freshmen's dormitory. One of the ironies of the event is that Graves Hall sits on one of the battlefields of the civil war, where Confederates attempted to hold back Sherman's advance to Atlanta. Years later, the area became home to Morehouse College, which hosted the funeral services of the leader of the crusade to tear down the walls of segregation, brick by brick. I could not help but reflect that I had routinely and recently walked in this place as a student.

The task of eulogizing Martin Luther King Jr. fell, appropriately, on the shoulders of Dr. Benjamin Mays, his mentor. My mother and I watched in utter silence as the television commentator announced that Dr. Mays, the president of Morehouse College, was about to step to the podium.

The voice that I had heard on so many occasions began in measured tones.

> To be honored by being requested to give the Eulogy at the funeral of Dr. Martin Luther King Jr., is like being asked to eulogize a deceased son—so close and so precious he was to me. Our friendship goes back to his student days at Morehouse College. It is not an easy task; nevertheless, I accept it, with a sad heart, and with full knowledge of my inadequacy to do justice to this man.

His eulogy, by preaching standards, is long. Dr. Mays knew that the world was watching and hanging onto every word. He sought to set the record straight and to speak to the minds and hearts of Americans and to every citizen of the world. He knew that his words would not be forgotten.

Dr. Lawrence Carter, Dean of the Martin Luther King Jr. International Chapel on the Morehouse campus and a Mays scholar, in the many discussions we had in his office, described May's preaching style as mystical, as well as keenly rhetorical.

> The content and cadence are blended to create in the audience a transformed state. Although he had a PhD in theology, he studied the uneducated preachers in his native South Carolina—who while preaching the Christian gospel retained the rhythm and spirituality of their native Africa.

"Mays will hook you," Dean Carter says.

And so, as Dr. Mays advanced toward his final words, he challenged the nation.

> I close by saying to you what Martin Luther King believed: If physical death was the price he had to pay to rid America of prejudice and injustice, nothing could be more redemptive. To paraphrase the words of the immortal John Fitzgerald Kennedy, "Martin Luther King Jr.'s unfinished work on earth must truly be our own."

When Dr. Mays concluded, my mother and I wept openly. "It is up to the living to carry on," he said. "This work is unfinished." I knew that my role in this human drama was to succeed and excel at whatever I pursued. That's what Dr. Mays would have expected me to do.

Within a few months, the high emotions of the assassination had moderated, and I was confronted with my own reality.

On August 26, 1968, my first son, Ronald Jr., was born. Pat had delayed her enrollment at the university. Although we had scraped along on graduate student pay, we had the support of two sets of grandparents. I was reclassified by the selective service, which lowered my chances of being drafted. I could relax a little.

One night, Pat and I decided to join the psychocultural revolution that had slowly ignited in the black community. This shift in thought about our history, literature, clothing, hair, and aspects of cultural self-determination was described by the scholar Molefe Asanti as "Afrocentricity," and it coincided with the movement for equal rights. We decided to purchase afro picks and comb our hair to create large afros. In addition, we each wore an African dashiki—a brightly colored, loose-fitting shirt made from African fabric. We felt a sense of cultural pride as a result of our transformation, and we decided to go out to one of the local night spots to "strut our stuff." I am not sure of Pat's experience, but I felt a new sense of assurance. We proclaimed that we were no longer ashamed of our African ancestry or our differences from the dominant majority. While changes in hair and dress were important cultural symbols, the transition struck at the heart of feelings of inferiority.

My parents were not ashamed of their Africanness. Their generation did not necessarily make cultural choices, but they attempted to become acculturated within the mainstream of American society in terms of dress and other manifestations. I sought to understand my feelings of estrangement from the dominant culture. My friend Ben Berry recommended I read *Souls of Black Folk*, by W. E. B. Du Bois who, in 1903, first revealed this "double consciousness" as a stressor in the black American's psychology. He observed keenly the divided consciousness of American blacks.

> It is a peculiar sensation, this double-consciousness, this sense of always looking at one's self through the eyes of others, of measuring one's soul by the tape of a world that looks on in amused contempt and pity. One ever feels his two-ness—an American, a Negro; two souls, two thoughts, two unreconciled strivings; two warring ideals in one dark body, whose dogged strength alone keeps it from being torn asunder.

At one extreme, this unresolved contradiction leads to self-hate, self-doubt, withdrawal, and rage; at the other, assimilationism, resignation, and emulation. I understood the importance of coming to terms with these opposite pulls within my own consciousness in order to achieve balance and a healthy identity. Today, in the age of Obama, many in the black community have made progress in this regard; however, for many others, this painful contradiction remains an unresolved issue.

Although I was deeply concerned about weighty psychological and cultural matters, my work at the university required total dedication to the pursuit of science. As I gained confidence, I was aware of doubters among those faculty members who believed that I was only at the university because of affirmative action, not because of academic merit. I was determined to prove, beyond any doubt, that I was as capable as any other student in the graduate program and perhaps more so.

During the summer, I decided to develop a method to organize my thoughts in a way that would allow me to excel academically. I had passed all my courses, but I wanted to do more than pass; my goal was to get the highest score in the class. One of my mother's favorite sayings is, "There is nothing like a clear understanding." How could I translate her down-to-earth wisdom into academic success?

During my first year at USF, I improved my ability to take notes in class. I had experimented with various ways to rewrite my notes. However, I had not designed a foolproof method. Dr. Winslow Caughey, nationally recognized expert on hemoglobin, was recruited by USF to develop a research program and to teach biochemistry. I was determined to do well in his course. During the summer, I worked to fine-tune the method that I meant to use in his class. Dr. Caughey's lecture style was easy to follow. He was very organized and detail-oriented and, like Dr. Hunter and Dr. Betz, emphasized experimental approaches that supported concepts and theories. I took detailed notes in a ring binder and used a variety of colored pens. Although his lectures were outlined, I carefully identified main topics and subtopics, observing the rules of outlining. Definitions were highlighted in a different color from context. I rewrote my notes in a separate binder. In the process, I attempted to avoid including anything that I did not understand. In fact, I used corroborative sources, text, and research articles to improve my understanding and to supplement rewritten notes. Of course, present-day computerization makes this methodology even more powerful.

Integration of the additional material into my notes provided an expanded, varied, and unique view of the subject matter. Another self-designed rule was to complete the process of rewriting my notes before the next class. In order to study for an exam, I started from rewritten notes. I created a skeleton outline from the notes and attempted to fill in the outline, writing from memory. When satisfied that my notes could be reproduced with the slightest of prompts, I knew I was ready for the exam. The method involved a great deal of writing. However, I have learned that memory is reinforced by writing rather than by simply reading. Often, when studying, students need a method that will discipline them to make optimal use of their time and effort.

Results of my new design for study were very satisfying. I began to earn the highest scores in biochemistry, one of the most difficult courses. As each exam was returned, Dr. Caughey indicated the individual who earned the highest mark. On most of the exams, the highest mark was earned by either me or a gangly redheaded fellow who was acknowledged as one of the brightest graduate students in the school. The experience boosted my confidence. One day during the spring of my second year, the dean of the Graduate School at the University of Florida visited USF for recruitment purposes. I was informed of his visit and given an audience. He had heard of my success in biochemistry and wanted me to consider a transfer to the PhD program at the University of Florida. Since the University of Florida's program was more established than the one at USF, I was eager to speak with him. He described the benefits of transferring and added that my admission would be contingent on the Graduate Record Exam.

"Ah, is this facilitative, or another roadblock?" I thought. After my acceptance to two graduate programs, which required the GRE, I felt the requirement to be unreasonable and decided not to apply.

Dan Sheehan, a fellow graduate student at USF, had transferred to an innovative PhD program under the auspices of the University of Tennessee, located in the National Laboratory at Oak Ridge. I had known Dan, a short stocky fellow, slightly balding, with shoulder-length hair, who was a pretty good guitar player. Dan was also respected by the faculty for his intellect and ability.

I received a call from Dan, who said that he had spoken to Dr. Clint Fuller, Director of the Graduate School at Oak Ridge, and that Dr. Fuller would like to meet me. Dan asked if I would fly up to Oak Ridge to meet with the director and a few faculty members. I was familiar with the school at Oak Ridge, and I remembered all the fuss over Dan when he was accepted. He assured me that in this once-in-a-lifetime opportunity, I would be in an exclusive group of about twelve students accepted each year from the best schools in the nation. He added, "By the way, you would be the first African American to be admitted." I was less intrigued about the possibility of being the first than I was about the chance to be in an environment where science was practiced by world-class scientists.

Colleges and universities were slowly adjusting to the presence of blacks on campuses, particularly in the South; however, many of the attitudes of the bygone era were still in place. At that time, Tennessee, one of the former Confederate states, was perceived as reluctant to integrate. My dad reminded me that Tennessee had an active Ku Klux Klan, especially in the rural areas. In spite of those social realities, however, he encouraged me to pursue the opportunity.

To get to Oak Ridge, I flew into Knoxville. The airport is situated in a valley surrounded by mountains, which makes landing an interesting experience. Oak Ridge is in the eastern part of the state, about twenty-five miles west of Knoxville. Dan picked me up from the airport and gave me a briefing on the school and the town. We stopped by his house to freshen up and drove to the reception planned for me at a faculty member's house. The reception was attended by core faculty as well as a few students. I was overwhelmed at their positive reaction. I later learned that I had been thoroughly checked out before my arrival. Meeting me in person was the final test. One consideration in my favor, which persuaded the director and faculty that I could handle the program, was a recommendation from Dr. Caughey, my biochemistry professor at USF.

I returned to Tampa. Within a few weeks, I had received an offer from the Graduate School of Biomedical Sciences at Oak Ridge to join the PhD program. I was awarded a tuition-free scholarship, a generous stipend for living expenses, and the promise of a free two-bedroom apartment. The decision to accept, from my point of view, was an easy one. However, it was a bad time for my household to move. Since Pat was expecting our second child, we decided that I would take the furniture in a U-Haul, along with my Volkswagen, and they would join me later.

Oak Ridge

— 14 —

It takes someone with a vision of the possibilities to attain new levels of experience, someone with the courage to live his dreams.

Les Brown

Oak Ridge is one of the few cities created because of a war. In 1939, in a letter to President Franklin Roosevelt, Albert Einstein warned him that the Germans were working on a dangerous new weapon with immense destructive power. President Roosevelt convinced Congress to fund secretly four locations to work on a similar weapon—Oak Ridge was one of the sites. The Oak Ridge experiments successfully produced the fissional material for the atomic bomb. In 1945, bombs were dropped on Hiroshima and Nagasaki, ending the war with Japan.

After the war, buildings and facilities used to develop the atomic bomb were transformed into laboratories for biological research, particularly research that involved radiation biology. A cadre of scientists, leaders in their fields, was recruited to Oak Ridge. The Biology Division was distinguished as among the best in the world for cutting-edge research in the biological sciences. A close relationship between the Oak Ridge Biology Division and the

University of Tennessee in Knoxville resulted; in 1965, the UT-Oak Ridge Graduate School of Biomedical Sciences was established.

On the day I arrived in Oak Ridge, nervous with excitement and expectation, I pulled my U-Haul into the parking lot next to my new apartment. My apartment was in one of the refurbished structures built during the war. Dan had asked some students to help me unload. Within a few hours, I was completely moved in. Most of the graduate students lived in similarly renovated structures within the same general area.

The first day at the laboratory, I obtained necessary security clearances and oriented myself to a building that, to my mind, resembled the inside of the *Star Trek* spaceship, the *Enterprise*. Most everyone wore white coats, and each floor was full of laboratories and equipment.

The offices of the Graduate School were on the third floor. Dr. Clint Fuller welcomed me to the school, as Dr. Long had welcomed me to USF. I was struck by the similarity of his demeanor and attitude to Dr. Long's. For a minute, I was lulled into a false sense of security.

"Ron, we have been anticipating your arrival for a few days now. How was the drive up from Florida?"

"Uneventful," I said, attempting to appear calm and collected. After introductions to the office staff, Dr. Fuller informed me, "In a few days, after you have settled, we are going to give you an oral exam in biochemistry. This will be for placement purposes, to see where you need to start with this important subject matter."

"What!" I said to myself. "An oral exam in biochemistry?" The words echoed in my mind.

"You might want to brush up in advance," he said. "Two of our senior scientists will ask you a variety of questions covering many topics in biochemistry. You will be allowed to use the blackboard to explain your answers."

"Well," I thought, "the blackboard is going to be a big help."

For the next few days, I immersed myself in biochemistry. To my benefit, I had recently completed a three-course sequence in biochemistry, and I was surprised by the amount I had retained. The exam lasted about two hours. I answered a variety of questions on fundamental concepts and theories in biochemistry. I did not just pass; I was exempted from biochemistry.

The black community in Oak Ridge, about 10 percent of the population, mostly lived in the segregated community of Scarboro, a few miles northwest of the city. The original residents had moved to Oak Ridge to work in the plants during the war. Oak Ridge High School held a proud history as the first high school in the South to be desegregated voluntarily in 1955, just a year after the Supreme Court ruled against school segregation in 1954. The city was a federal enclave rather than a self-governed municipality, and the transition occurred without much fanfare and without the violence that accompanied the integration of the high school in Clinton, Tennessee, a few miles from Oak Ridge.

A few months after I arrived, the city was buzzing with news of an incident that had resulted in the suspension of the entire black student body of Oak Ridge High School. Black students had received permission to commemorate the assassination of Dr. King with a bulletin board that depicted important events in the civil rights struggle. When the students returned to school the next day, the bulletin board had been defaced. Black students quickly assembled and staged a sit-in in the lobby of the school. The principal asked them to leave the lobby or face suspension. The students refused and were summarily suspended. The local NAACP called a meeting for the following evening at the community center in Scarboro, which I attended. Because I was somewhat outspoken at the meeting, I was asked to participate in a small committee to approach the school system with a list of grievances articulated by the students and parents. The list included complaints that transcended the defaced bulletin board and encompassed, in general, biased treatment of black students by teachers and administrators at the school.

Our committee succeeded in getting the students reinstated. We also encouraged the superintendent and principal to agree to a series of sensitivity training workshops for a select group of parents and teachers. The sessions were facilitated by faculty in the Department of Education at the University of Tennessee. The workshops were designed to bring together school personnel and members of the black community to discuss problems at the school and to develop strategies for change. The strategy worked because the white administrators and teachers and black community leaders and parents agreed to talk honestly and openly about preconceived attitudes about race, which included racial stereotypes. While not all of the racial problems were solved, significant goodwill was generated, along with a commitment to work together to avoid future problems.

Then I reminded myself that I was not a community activist but a graduate student. Plus, in the midst of all of the work for racial conciliation, Pat delivered a baby girl on October 4, 1969. We named her Lisa. I thought, "What a blessing," and I looked forward to seeing them at the Christmas break for the move to Oak Ridge. In January, Pat and the kids joined me.

In addition to the coursework, prior to choosing a thesis topic, one of the requirements was to rotate through three laboratories in order to make a selection. I chose Drs. Don and Ada Olins, who had pioneered work on chromatin structure and function; Dr. Jane Setlow, a leading authority on DNA repair; and Dr. Roy Curtiss III, an acknowledged expert on conjugation in bacteria.

Each laboratory experience was intriguing; however, I remember a conversation with Dr. Setlow as she and I reviewed data one evening. She asked why I wanted to become a scientist. In her opinion, problems in the black community cried out for leadership of a different sort. She thought I had more of an interest in community leadership after my brief involvement and notoriety with the high school incident. Initially, I was taken aback that my motivation was questioned. I responded with a cryptic comment.

Dr. Roy Curtiss, III

"Dr. Setlow," I said, "you don't know me." I learned a great deal in her laboratory and held her in high regard as a scientist; however, we agreed to disagree about my future.

After the experience in Dr. Curtiss's laboratory, I decided that I wanted to work in his area of expertise, microbial genetics, and that I liked his laid-back style.

Roy Curtiss was tall and slender. He had a wry sense of humor and a disarming intelligence that saw connections when colleagues and students were stumped. When we discussed possibilities for my thesis research, he provided a number of options.

"Ron, I want you to look over this notebook, which contains ideas for future projects based on what we have done and are doing in this lab. All you have to do is choose one—the ideas are all laid out."

He wasn't prepared for my response. "Roy, if you don't mind, I would like to develop a few ideas of my own that would form the basis for my thesis problem."

I suspected he thought my comeback was either the height of naïveté or one of the boldest statements he had ever heard from a student. To his credit, he didn't throw me out of his office, but simply said, "Okay, why don't you have at it?" While I got my wish, quite frankly, I was not completely on my own. Roy's lab was deeply involved in work that attempted to explain the molecular mechanisms of bacterial conjugation (sex in bacteria).

The study of sex in bacteria, on the face of it, appears rather exotic. The small DNA molecules or genetic determinants responsible for maleness in bacteria are called plasmids. These small molecules reside in the cytoplasm of male bacterial cells. A female bacterium, by definition, does not have a plasmid. A female bacterium that

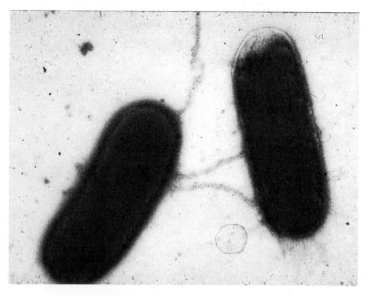

Conjugating Bacteria (The male is on the left,
filaments between them are pili)

receives a plasmid through the conjugal act becomes a male. The
medical importance of plasmids is that they often contain genes
that allow the bacterium to resist antibiotics. Because plasmids can
be transferred from one bacterium to another, resistance can expand
in populations of bacteria, which further complicates treatment of
an infection. Before the advent of antibiotics, millions of people
died from what we consider to be common infections—wounds
and venereal disease are examples. A world in which antibiotics
are ineffective would be catastrophic for humans. Therefore, an
understanding of every aspect of the biology of plasmids is essential
if we are to control the acquisition of antibiotic resistance among
microorganisms and ultimately save lives. Curtiss, the acknowledged
leader in the field, had recently written a review on the subject.

During the summers, the Biology Division developed a program
to bring undergraduates from various colleges and universities to
the lab for a hands-on research experience. For two consecutive
summers, I was assigned an undergraduate trainee. Both were from
historically black colleges. Clifton Orr, from Mary Holmes College

in West Point, Mississippi, was my trainee the first summer. Cliff was energetic, smart, and inquisitive. I had just begun my thesis research, and we worked together every day for about six weeks.

We demonstrated that a certain plasmid found in the bacterium *Salmonella typhimurium* was unstable and separated into two units. Eventually we isolated these molecules. With the help of Dave Allison, an electron microscope technician at the lab, we were able to take pictures of the molecules. Our work was eventually published in the *Journal of Bacteriology*, and the phenomenon has since been confirmed by other laboratories. I was proud to include Cliff's name as one of the authors. A few years later, he enrolled in the Biomedical School at Oak Ridge. The next summer, my undergraduate trainee was Anderson Perry from Tennessee State University in Nashville. Anderson was bright but, unlike Cliff, quiet and withdrawn. He was obviously uncomfortable around whites and only spoke to answer questions. I recognized his insecurity and was very patient with him. I knew that if I could motivate him to ask questions, he would be hooked as I was, years before, in Dr. Hunter's classes. One day, as they say, out of the blue, Anderson looked up from his work and said, "So, Ron, how are we going to prove there is a barrier to DNA transfer between two male cells?"

"Well, Anderson," I said, hoping to hide my surprised reaction to this welcome query, "we are going to use mini-cell producing cells to our advantage, since we can separate them from normal-sized cells after mating." The mini-cell is a cell division mutant which, instead of dividing down the middle as do normal cells, divides at the ends to produce mini-cells. "If we can show that mini-cells, derived from male producing cells, exclude DNA in matings with normal-sized male cells when compared to mini-cells derived from female cells, we might be on to something."

He said, "Huh," and went back to his work. From that point, he wanted to know every move I made with an explanation. We conclusively established the phenomenon, which we termed "entry exclusion." Additionally, we predicted that the barrier to the transfer of DNA between male cells operated at the cell membrane, which was later confirmed by other laboratories. The work was eventually published in the *Journal of Bacteriology*, and Anderson Perry is listed as one of the authors. On his last day in Oak Ridge, Anderson stopped by my apartment to say good-bye.

"Ron," he said, "I want to thank you for hanging in there with me. I doubted at first that we could do this, but you showed me the possibilities."

I felt that I had been a good role model for Cliff and Anderson, but where was my role model? Practically every day of the week, a seminar was presented at the lab by either one of the resident scientists or an invited guest. Since only a handful of black scientists were considered worthy of an invitation to present at Oak Ridge, I rarely saw one. Finally, I learned that Dr. Luther Williams, a professor at Purdue University, was scheduled to offer a seminar. Dr. Williams, short in stature and with a self-assured glint in his eye, was a few years older than I. He supervised an active laboratory that investigated the control of biochemical reactions within cells. After his seminar, I waited until the questions ended and he had a free moment.

"Dr. Williams, I am Ron Sheehy. I'm in the graduate school here, and I really enjoyed your seminar."

"I know who you are," he said, "Clint Fuller can't stop bragging about you."

"Well, if you aren't doing anything later, why don't you stop by my apartment, and we can sort of compare notes, if you know what I mean?"

He said, "Okay, I'll see you around seven PM."

When we sat down over a pint of Old Taylor, we were like two aliens from outer space meeting each other on Earth for the first time. We joked and laughed like inmates who are surprised to find they are in the same asylum. Luther knew the "scientific game." He was an accomplished researcher with considerable political skills. As he began to talk, I sat on the edge of my chair.

"Ron, you need to understand that science is not unlike the corporate world. It's very competitive, and there is a hierarchy within your field. Success is not always based on merit, but on who you know and who you were trained by. The leading laboratories in certain specialized areas compete, but they also exchange data and share the latest results. If you are not in this information loop or are not invited to certain meetings, you are out of the game. You either publish or perish, and I might add that you have to publish in the 'right' journals. You won't find many who look like you in this field, but you have to persevere." Then he continued.

"Ron, you're in a position to crack the ceiling. Your next move is to do a post doctorate with a prominent researcher in your field, which will position you to land an appointment at a major university. The appointment will come with start-up money for your research and a decent salary."

As Luther painted a picture of my future, I thought, "Wow, how am I going to do all of this?"

After a year of the frustrations and challenges of maintaining family life in a remote city without relatives, Pat and the kids returned to Tampa. She was more comfortable in the friendly confines of Tampa, where she had the support of grandparents. Although terribly disappointed, I renewed my concentration on work at the lab.

Middle Tennessee seemed to have its share of gray days during the winter, and we celebrated when the sun peeked through the mostly overcast skies. Occasionally we enjoyed snowfall, which broke the monotony of the barren landscape. Socially, we were limited to the bar at the local Holiday Inn, which was a favorite weekend spot, or I drove over to Scarboro, referred to as "the Valley." Two establishments were on my itinerary. Dewey's was a restaurant that offered a pig's feet sandwich and other delicacies. Next door, the Paradise Club featured a rhythm and blues band. This rather large room with a fairly long bar, a few tables and chairs, and a big potbelly stove in the rear corner was mostly deserted on the nights the band did not perform. When out of diversions on a Friday night, Oak Ridge was a pretty lonely place, and I missed my family.

Music was one consolation. I developed the habit of stopping by the local record store, after a long week at the lab, to check out the latest releases. I usually purchased three or four albums. As a regular customer, I got to know the clerk in the record store and counted on his advice on good music.

"Hey, Jack, I want something tonight with an upbeat tempo. What do you have?"

"Well, Ron, do you like Marvin Gaye? He has a new release. We just got it in. I haven't listened to it, but you remember he used to be with Motown."

"Oh, yes, he and Tammi Terrell made a few records together. I haven't been following his career, but he was a pretty good singer, as I recall."

Jack was never a hard-pressure salesman. He said matter-of-factly, "The album is titled *What's Going On*. Look in the rhythm and blues section."

"Are you sure about this, Jack? You haven't listened to it, and yet you want me to buy it with a no-return policy."

"Well, you can pass on it and check out some Bobby Womack or Little Johnny Taylor, both of whom have new releases."

"Okay, I'll take a chance on Marvin Gaye, but also give me the new release by Womack."

I can't say I paid much attention to Marvin Gaye's album initially. I put it on the stereo, and I settled in for the night. Initially the music caught my attention, and then the lyrics. I listened carefully as the music filled my apartment. The first two songs, from the point of view of a Vietnam veteran who had returned home from war, contemplated the senselessness of war, injustice, poverty and racism—a creative critical response to what was happening in the country in 1971. The rest of the album contained songs about the destruction of the environment, drug abuse, political corruption, and faith in God. These profound statements, combined with great music, captured my generation's concerns and touched a chord in my soul, unlike any other music. I immediately called all my buddies to tell them I had discovered something special and that they should drop what they were doing and come over to my apartment. We listened for hours, as if we were in church. Not surprisingly, *What's Going On* is considered a landmark recording in pop music history and one of the greatest albums ever made.

Most PhD programs have a series of qualifying examinations that test the student over the broad outlines of the discipline. Instead of exams, we were required to develop two research projects. They had to include a research idea or proposal, the experimental approach, and probable results. The exercise nearly drove me to enroll in law school. I became convinced that studying law would be a more direct way to contribute to the struggle for equal opportunity— the original suggestion of Dr. Setlow—rather than the pursuit of science in the research lab. I allowed fatigue and doubt to control my thoughts, and I called for an appointment with the Law School dean at the University of Tennessee's Law School in Knoxville. He granted me an appointment and was very supportive during our conversation. I thought that, given my status as a graduate student, I could waltz into the Law School. How naïve I was! Toward the end of our conversation, he said, "I want you to take the LSAT, and based on your score, we will talk further." On my drive back to Oak Ridge, sanity returned, and I started to think of research ideas for the proposals. I successfully completed two proposals and passed my qualifiers.

I could see the light at the end of the tunnel in my final year. George Kachatourian, a Canadian who was originally from Armenia, joined Roy's lab as a post doctorate fellow. George and I hit it off immediately. We collaborated on a series of experiments on the "Fate of Conjugally Transferred DNA in the Mini-cells," which was published in the *Journal of Molecular General Genetics* and was the final chapter in my PhD dissertation.

In a telephone conversation with Pat, I learned that our differences, which had been building over the previous year, were irreconcilable. Too often, young people become overwhelmed with the responsibilities of career and children; our relationship succumbed to the stress. We were not strong enough or mature enough to weather the stresses and strains. George and his wife consoled me during this difficult time, and work became an escape from a broken heart.

The final requirement of the PhD program, before turning in the dissertation, was to give a major seminar about one's research and its conclusions. My seminar was scheduled during the spring of my final year. Senior scientists, staff, and technicians at the lab attended. After the presentation, I fielded questions from the audience. I am certain Roy Curtiss was as relieved as I was when it was over. I returned to my apartment around 5:00 PM. I lay on the couch to recuperate from the stressful day. When I awoke, I was surprised to learn it was 7:00 AM the next morning. This was an example of stress-induced sleep. I had internalized a significant amount of stress.

One day, while Ken Roosen, one of Roy's graduate students, and I talked about the trials and tribulations of graduate school, the phone in the lab rang.

The operator asked, "Is this Ron Sheehy?"

I said, "Yes, it is."

"I am transferring a call from Dr. Philip Hartman. Will you take the call?"

I immediately recognized the name as one of the leading microbial geneticists in the country. "Yes," I said, "put him through."

"Ron, this is Phil Hartman from Johns Hopkins. We would like to invite you to give a seminar in our department. Of course, we will pick up all the expenses. Just let me know when you can come, and I will make all of the arrangements."

Trying to maintain my composure, I said, "Of course, I'll get back with you. Thanks for calling."

Ken had overheard parts of the conversation and asked, "What was that all about?"

"I've just been invited to give a seminar at Johns Hopkins," I said. Later that day, I found Roy Curtiss in his office and told him about the invitation.

He said, without showing any astonishment, "They must want to consider you for an appointment in the department."

I was flattered, but the reality was that I had not completed the PhD. Nor had I done the requisite post doctorate. No matter! I accepted the invitation.

I arrived in Baltimore and was picked up at the airport by Dr. Hartman. He had an easygoing manner that made me feel comfortable right away. On the ride to the university, he described the department of biology and the arrangements for my seminar at noon. My impression was that the invitation was his idea and that he and unnamed colleagues sought to recruit an African American faculty member. When we arrived at the university, we stopped by his office, where he introduced me to members of the graduate faculty, as well as graduate students. The offices and laboratories on his floor appeared cramped for space, and I could tell the environment was intense. The final introduction was with Dr. Saul Roseman, the department chair, who, Hartman forewarned me, could be "a little direct."

The noon hour quickly approached. I decided to talk about the "entry exclusion" research. Although I had recently presented the talk at a regional meeting of the American Society for Microbiology, I was a bit nervous as the time for the seminar approached. We met in a classroom that barely accommodated all of the faculty and students. As the room filled, the chairs were quickly taken, and students began to sit on the floor right in front of me. I was introduced by Dr. Hartman, who told the audience that I was a PhD candidate in Roy Curtiss's lab. The impact of hearing this made me think about Luther Williams's advice on the value and prestige of the professional mentor. With formalities out of the way, I began.

Toward the end, Dr. Roseman interrupted me mid-sentence. "How do you know that is DNA?" I was stunned. The question struck me as similar to asking a person who is holding a stick, "How do you know that is wood?"

As I regained my composure, I said, "It's labeled with a radioactive compound specific for DNA." Of course, the question was not a serious one. To this day, I am not sure what it was intended to accomplish. I returned to Oak Ridge, relieved that my brief excursion into the world that Luther Williams had described was over. The experience was sobering and somewhat stressful. A few weeks later, I received a call from Dr. Hartman to thank me. I felt his effort to let me down gently when he uttered the words, "We are not going to make an offer." He added, "You have a bright future ahead of you, and I recommend you do a postdoc." I knew I needed to get busy and find a laboratory for my postdoctorate experience.

I contacted two of the leading researchers in the country who studied plasmids: Dr. Roy Clowes at the University of Texas at Dallas and Dr. Richard Novick at the Public Health Research Institute in New York. Both offered me positions, which included a decent salary and moving expenses. I decided that New York was more interesting than Dallas and accepted the offer from Novick. I am sure that I wouldn't have gotten to first base without Roy Curtiss's recommendation. I was sure that the offers were not based on affirmative action because no lab would waste a postdoc appointment on someone who could not contribute right away.

Writing my PhD dissertation was straightforward, since the majority of the research results had been previously published in referred journals. I asked Dan Sheehan's wife, Linda, an experienced typist, to retype the papers and assemble them into an official document. I proofed the document and incorporated comments from Curtiss. I felt no compelling desire to participate in the graduation ceremonies at the University of Tennessee and did not return to Tennessee for the occasion. I received notice from the University, while in New York, that my PhD was awarded on December 8, 1972.

I packed all my belongings either inside or on top of my Volkswagen in preparation to leave Oak Ridge for New York. As I crossed the Clinch River Bridge, I pulled over and stepped outside. I looked back at the bridge and the two-lane highway that led into the city of Oak Ridge. I could see the Y-12 plant, which houses the Biology Division, in the distance from the highway. The building is a five-story, windowless, dark red structure surrounded by fences and barbed wire.

"What an intimidating building," I thought. Yet for three years, it had been my incubator, where I spent untold hours as a graduate student and where I learned to be a professional scientist who thought primarily about research. So many relationships were established, both in the lab and in the city. I would miss Oak Ridge.

Y-12 Building (Biology Division), Oak Ridge National Laboratory

New York

— 15

How I managed to cross the Hudson River Bridge and not lose the stuff on top of my Volkswagen is beyond me. Richard Novick had offered to put me up for a few nights. A block from his residence on Central Park West, I looked in the rearview mirror and saw the luggage rack halfway down the back of my car. I had stopped to push the rack back in place when Novick rode by on his bicycle.

He slowed down. "Looks like you have that under control. My apartment is in the next block. I'll be back in about thirty minutes. Our housekeeper is expecting you."

The streets were jammed with cars, yellow cabs, the sounds of honking horns, and people of every description and ethnicity. This was September of 1972, and New Yorkers were enjoying the good weather before the onslaught of winter. I had lived in the hills of Tennessee for three years, and I felt like a duck out of water. Novick's housekeeper was not overly friendly and did not offer to make life easy for me. I decided not to stay with Novick. I knew that if I could get to a phone, I could call a Morehouse classmate to come and help me. I needed to store my things and find an apartment; however, my more immediate need was a place to sleep for the night.

I finally contacted my friend, Harold Ingram, who offered his floor for the night and a secure place to park my car. Harold lived in Harlem, on the fifteenth floor of a high-rise just off Lenox Avenue. Harold, whom we called "Sage" because of his quiet and cerebral manner, lived in a one-room flat. I slept on his floor for two weeks; then I moved into an apartment in Bethune Towers on 143rd Street in Harlem.

Public Health Research Institute, New York

The Public Health Research Institute, a private, nonprofit institute, was founded by the city as a venue for basic research on infectious diseases. The facility was located in a building on the corner of First and Twenty-first streets on the Lower East Side. Novick's laboratories were on the tenth floor of a fifteen-story building. The first day, he introduced me to his staff and showed me around the laboratory. Everything looked familiar except the view from windows in the laboratory, views that included the Empire State Building.

At the end of the day, I walked outside to discover that my car was not where I had left it. In the grip of a panic attack, I surveyed the street, thinking that I had forgotten where I parked. My second thought was that someone had stolen it. Then the guard in the building, who had noticed my bewilderment, volunteered that the car had been towed by a police wrecker. He said my bumper was in the "no-parking" zone, denoted by a yellow mark on the curb. Well, welcome to New York. This was not Oak Ridge, I discovered in a hurry.

I decided to take the subway from Harlem to work. To get to the East Side, I needed to take—as they say in New York—two trains. I transferred from one train to another. The problem with this strategy was that by the time I arrived at work, my brain was so jostled from the train ride that I couldn't calm down until after lunch. I reconsidered and drove every day. The constant problem of finding a parking space was preferable to the subway.

Dr. Richard Novick

Richard Novick was short in stature. He had a prominent, bushy mustache and thick, brown hair, which he parted and brushed to one side. He was born and raised in New York City. In his speech and his demeanor, he was quick and impatient; he behaved like a prototypical New Yorker. Novick was, however, an atypical biomedical scientist.

He was trained as an MD, and his postdoctoral experiences after medical school took place in basic research laboratories. In another break with convention, instead of studying antibiotic resistance in *Escherichia coli*—the microorganism of choice at the time—Novick pioneered the study of antibiotic resistance in *Staphylococcus*. *Staphylococcus* is a bacterium frequently found in the nose and on the skin. It can cause a range of illnesses, from minor infections to life-threatening diseases such a pneumonia and meningitis. *Staphylococcus* is a major cause of hospital infections in America and throughout the world. The treatment of choice for *Staphylococcus* is antibiotics. However, the bacterium has become resistant to various commonly used antibiotics. The importance of understanding the basic biology of antibiotic resistance in this organism and the discovery of effective treatments cannot be overemphasized.

Novick discovered that in *Staphylococcus*, as in *E .coli*, the genes for antibiotic resistance are carried on plasmids. Before I joined his lab, Novick had begun to study the transmission of antibiotic resistance among staphylococcal strains and the replication and control of plasmid DNA in *Staphylococcus*. He was respected as one of the leaders in the field of plasmid studies in bacteria.

Our discussions about a proposed project focused on the control and replication of plasmid DNA in *Staphylococcus*. Plasmids, similar to a variety of viruses, replicate to maintain an existence in cells. As the bacteria divide, the plasmids produce copies of themselves for distribution into daughter cells. He showed me that the introduction of a short pulse (about thirty seconds) of radioactive thymidine, incorporated only into the DNA of a growing culture of bacteria, allowed the identification of replicative intermediates as units were added. The unfinished molecules were at various stages of completion. The technique was not new and had been successfully used to study DNA replication in viruses and a number of organisms. What was new was the attempt to identify replicative intermediates of plasmid DNA, which were masked by the much larger bacterial chromosome. Essentially, separating the plasmid molecules from the bacterial chromosome was the problem, akin to separating a marble embedded in a web of thread.

A few months passed with no apparent solution to the problem. The preferred technique was to separate the larger bacterial chromosome from the smaller plasmids on the basis of size. A technique pioneered at Oak Ridge was the separation of biological molecules on the basis of size and conformation in sucrose gradients. A gradient may consist of increasing concentrations of sucrose in 10 percent increments. The sample containing the molecules of interest is placed on top of the gradient and centrifuged at high speeds. The centrifugal force, acting as gravity, would pull (sediment) the molecules through the inert solution of sucrose. The larger the molecule, in general, the faster it would sediment. The chromosome was located as a pellet in the bottom of the tube, and the plasmids were distributed by size and conformation in the body of the tube.

Two innovations produced the result that we sought. Instead of "popping" the bacteria and then layering the contents on top of the sucrose gradient, the bacteria were "popped open" on top of the sucrose gradient. The result was a very gentle way to open the bacteria, avoiding breakage of the bacterial chromosome. The second innovation occurred after the tubes were spun in a centrifuge. The tubes were collected from the top instead of the bottom. Collection from the top made all the difference; however, initially, the reversal from bottom to top was not at all obvious. The laboratory equipment was designed for bottom collection.

The idea of collection from the top came from someone who was unfamiliar with any of the techniques and had no prejudices or history of commonly accepted practices. When I explained the problem to my lunch companion, a medical student doing research in another laboratory, she replied, "Why don't you collect from the top?" To rig an apparatus that slowly lowered a pipette into the top of the tube and extracted small, measured amounts at a time was the trick. I showed Novick the results, to his delight.

We were the first laboratory to demonstrate replicative intermediates of plasmid DNA molecules. After I had confirmed the initial results in further experiments, he came to me one day and asked me to join him for dinner. That evening with Novick and his wife, I received the greatest compliment. With a broad smile, he said "I wish I had done that experiment." He knew that we had opened a door to understanding the behavior of molecules that transmitted resistance to antibiotics.

Novick was in the process of organizing an invitation-only meeting of investigators in the area of plasmid molecular biology to be held in New Orleans. I was asked to present the results of our experiments. For a postdoc—not to mention an African American—to present at this kind of meeting was unusual. I was the only African American in the room. After the presentation, as I left the podium, I noticed a variety of expressions in the audience: disbelief, smiles of encouragement, and sheer incredulity.

It was 1973. We heard through the grapevine that Stanley Cohen and Herbert Boyer, in California, had succeeded in demonstrating that plasmid DNA could be cut with enzymes, which acted as scissors. Then DNA from a different source was inserted into the plasmid, and the combined plasmid was placed back into the bacterial cell. The discovery signaled the birth of genetic engineering. Using these techniques, the gene for insulin was combined with plasmid DNA to produce the first synthetic insulin, which promised to ease the undersupply of insulin from animal sources. Later Boyer founded Genentech, a major biotechnology corporation, with venture capitalist Robert Swanson.

The interest in plasmid biology and genetic engineering had skyrocketed, and we in the field worked to think of innovative and unique applications for the new technology. I was at a crossroads. I could continue to work with Novick to extend studies on plasmid replication or look for jobs in academia or industry. One day the laboratory phone rang, and on the other end was Dr. Thomas Norris, who identified himself as chairman of the biology department at Morehouse College.

"Dr. Sheehy," he said, "I'll be in New York over the weekend, and I would like to come by and talk with you." He informed me up front that he was white, and I told him that I lived in Harlem. He responded, "No problem, what is your address?"

When I heard the buzzer, I turned on my intercom. "Is that you, Dr. Norris?"

A nervous voice answered, "I think you need to hurry and let me in."

I understood his apprehension. Harlem was not exactly a danger-free zone for whites. I am not sure what I expected. Tom Norris was short, with a full beard and almost shoulder-length hair, and he reminded me immediately of Kenny Rogers, the country and western singer. Tom said he was trained as a biochemist and had been hired at Morehouse a few years earlier to teach biochemistry. Recently, however, the president had named him head of the department. He got right to the point.

"You know, Dr. Sheehy, we desperately need you to return to Morehouse."

"Tom," I said, "please call me Ron."

I hoped to relax him a bit. "That's a tall proposition. I like my work in research, and a move to Morehouse would sacrifice that career goal." Norris adjusted his seat and leaned forward to make his point. He said, "We would provide you with start-up funds and a newly renovated laboratory."

"I remember Hope Hall," I said, "and I can't imagine how you could renovate that old building to create a first-class laboratory."

"If you will come, we will do it," he replied. I had to give him credit; he tried hard to convince me, even though his statements about facilities and resources were unconvincing. As we ended our conversation, I told him I would give the offer some thought and would get back to him within the month.

I broached the subject of my return to Morehouse with Novick. He didn't think the idea was good for me. He advised me to stay on track with my research and to consider a research professorship at a major university. I recognized the suggestion as one that could lead to a life-changing decision. Once I had made a commitment to Morehouse, a return to competitive science at majority institutions would be difficult. On the other hand, the thought crossed my mind: Could I do competitive science at Morehouse?

"Are you crazy? If you don't publish, you're out of the game," my muse said.

Okay, this is a risk, I thought; but I had an advantage. The method I had developed in Novick's lab was unique, and its potential had not been fully explored. Perhaps, if I initiated a study of replicating plasmid molecules in a different bacterial system, could I attract funding sources? I was intrigued with the possibility that I could create a competitive laboratory in an environment free of the distractions of race. I also reasoned that a successful demonstration at Morehouse, showing that we could compete with laboratories anywhere in the world, would be more meaningful than developing the same kind of laboratory at a predominantly white institution. I thought of Dr. May's admonition that "low aim was a sin." I also knew that a number of my former professors would still be there. Contemplation of the vast possibilities literally kept me up at night. Finally I made a decision. I called Tom Norris to tell him that I would join the department in December. I forgot to ask him about salary. I had made up my mind to follow my course, and salary was not an issue.

As I thought about this change in environment, I reflected on the events and people that had contributed to my development at a time when, as Dr. Mays had so eloquently put it at my graduation, "You are the most fortunate class that has ever graduated from Morehouse. Barriers of segregation are falling so fast that they make the timid and the insecure dizzy." I had taken advantage of opportunities, but I was also assisted by fair-minded individuals who saw potential and gave me the chance to succeed.

The Return to Morehouse

> Most people are not really free. They are confined by the niche in the world that they carve out for themselves. They limit themselves to fewer possibilities by the narrowness of their vision.

> **V. S. Naipaul**

I left New York, in December 1973, the way I had left Oak Ridge, with all my belongings packed either inside or on top of my Volkswagen. Tom had given me directions to his house in Atlanta. He and his wife lived in a fairly modest wood structure, set off the road and surrounded by woods, in southwest Atlanta. The couple had graciously extended an invitation to stay with them as long as I needed. I knew I would be more comfortable in an apartment of my own and, within a few days, had located an apartment in the Washington Road area near the airport.

My first day on campus, I was greeted by Dr. Hugh Morris Gloster, the president of the college, who had succeeded Dr. Mays. A Morehouse graduate, Dr. Gloster was the former academic dean at Hampton University in Virginia. He was relatively tall, which complemented a dignified bearing. For some reason, he took me on a walking tour of the campus, during which he pointed out buildings that I knew all too well. In any event, I appreciated his taking the time to welcome me. When the tour ended, he turned to me and said in his gravelly voice, "Dr. Sheehy, we are expecting great things from you. Dr. Norris says you are quite a biologist."

"I'll do my best," I said.

John Hope Hall, Morehouse College

John Hope Hall, which houses the biology department, is a three-story brick structure built around the turn of the century. Not much had changed since I was a student. Tom greeted me warmly and showed me the room he had proposed to renovate for my laboratory. Situated at the front of the building, the room provided adequate space and was blessed with large windows. I could see possibilities. The rest of the first floor was devoted to offices, a stock room, and a small laboratory that Tom had created for himself. The stock room, a dusty, dimly lit room, contained jars of embalmed specimens and turn-of-the-century equipment. The second and third floors contained additional offices and teaching laboratories.

"Well," I thought, "I'm going to need hundreds of thousands of dollars, if not millions, to pull this off."

True to his word and according to my specifications, Tom transformed the space into a first-class laboratory.

Although I was free of teaching responsibilities that spring semester, Dr. Frederick Mapp asked me to present a lecture on DNA in his genetics class. A classically trained biologist, Dr. Mapp was the previous chair of the department, and he had been chair when I was a student. His PhD degree was from the University of Chicago. At the end of my lecture, I was surprised and happy to discover, from the standing ovation, that the students were excited to hear about the new discoveries in biology. My spirits rose. Quite frankly, when I was an undergraduate student, Dr. Mapp—who believed in discipline and the "correct" way of doing things—reminded me of my fourth grade teacher, Mrs. Gibson. When I was a student, he said on several occasions, "Sheehy, you just won't listen." He mistook my independence as a challenge to his authority. This aspect of my character would bedevil me for years, beyond my career as a scientist. Because of my history with Dr. Mapp, the invitation to lecture in his class was very special indeed.

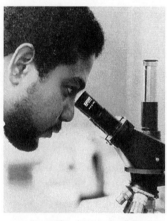

Ron Sheehy in the lab

During my first few years back at Morehouse, I successfully acquired a number of grants, which enabled me to outfit the laboratory. Substantial support for major equipment, centrifuges, and radioactive counters was also secured, as well as funds for technical support and training. Errol Archibald, a native Panamanian who was a PhD student under Luther Williams at Purdue, transferred to Atlanta University to finish his PhD studies. Archibald signed on as my first postdoc. He was a hard worker and a brilliant experimentalist. We accepted the responsibility to train four master's-level students from Atlanta University. I hired two full-time technicians and renovated the remaining space on the first floor to include a prep room, major equipment room, and a small computer room to input our data. The laboratory was taking shape.

Novick had been on my case to send a draft of the manuscript of work I had produced in New York. After a few revisions, the manuscript was accepted for publication in the *Journal of Molecular Biology*, one of the most prestigious journals in the field. The article appeared in April 1975. I was asked to teach a course in molecular biology for undergraduates and graduate students at Atlanta University. Clarence Clark, a Morehouse graduate who was completing his PhD at Atlanta University, decided to join our developing research group. Clarence had graduated ahead of me at Morehouse, and he brought maturity and a strong desire to succeed to his work. Right away he recognized our opportunity to produce significant research. To accommodate additional master-level students from Atlanta University, as well as a few undergraduates, we divided the mentorships and projects among the three of us. Because of the increased number of people at work on the first floor of Hope Hall, we frequently had a hard time staying out of each other's way. When we held research meetings to discuss the progress of various projects, the second-floor classroom was full. Centrifuges and radioactive counters operated around the clock, as active in the evening as during the day. The electrical system in Hope Hall was stressed to the breaking point, which caused regular outages.

Tom approached me one day. "Ron, I'm thinking about stepping down as chair to devote full time to assist in the development of the new Morehouse Medical School. I want to recommend you to replace me as chair."

I had mixed feelings. Our progress was well on the way on the research front, and I wondered if I could handle the administrative duties as chair of the biology department along with laboratory operations. Within days, I was summoned to the president's office for a meeting to discuss the proposition. President Gloster was seated at his desk, and to his right sat Dean Hubert. Tom and I occupied seats that faced the desk.

Tom opened the meeting in his methodical style. "Dr. Gloster, I've asked Dr. Sheehy to meet with us to discuss his taking over the chairmanship of the department. I am certain he will do a good job."

Dr. Gloster shifted in his seat. "I understand you are recently divorced. You think the young women are going to leave you alone so you can chair the department?" he asked with a chuckle. He and Dean Hubert traded sly smiles.

"I don't think that will be a problem," I said, in an attempt to defuse the bachelorhood issue and return the discussion to a serious tone.

"Well, we'll give this some thought and will be in touch with you," President Gloster said.

Wondering what to make of the discussion, I left. An hour later, Tom came to my office. "It's a done deal. You are now the chair, effective immediately."

The year of our debut as a research group was 1976. We had successfully isolated plasmid molecules in *E. coli*, using the technique I had developed in New York for *Staphylococcus*. The research was presented by one of our graduate students at a regional meeting of the American Society for Microbiology at the University of Georgia in Athens. Archibald and I were proud and elated that the research from Morehouse was well-received and that our student had made an excellent presentation.

The summer afforded me an opportunity to think about the curriculum for the biology department. I had recommended my colleagues, Archibald and Clarence, for faculty positions, and the department was growing in numbers of undergraduates. Traditionally, our undergraduates were interested in the health professions; very few contemplated a research career. The Office of Health Professions needed a director, and I began a search for a director who could teach a new course in cell biology. With the stroke of a pen, I changed the curriculum. New courses were added in cell biology, biochemistry, and anatomy and physiology. The latter two courses were taught by faculty assigned to the newly created Morehouse Medical School. Advanced courses in molecular

Morehouse students in Advanced Molecular Biology

biology and cellular genetics were added to ensure that students would be familiar with cutting-edge research. On the third floor of Hope Hall, we created a seminar room with large couches and cushioned chairs in a semicircle, a setting where students enrolled in advanced courses could present analyses of journal articles and critique research conclusions. Dialogue was encouraged among the students and between the students and me.

During this period, one student caught my attention. He was not enrolled at Morehouse; he attended Clark College, a coeducational institution across the street from Morehouse. Because of an agreement between the colleges, which allowed for cross registration, he took the molecular biology course that I taught. He sat near the rear of the classroom and often interrupted my lectures with, "Dr. Sheehy, how do you know that ...?" This is the most challenging kind of question for a teacher. However, I discovered that his intent was not to put me on the spot. Quite the contrary; he really wanted to know the evidence for my assertions. I supplied as much experimental evidence as I could muster to answer his questions. From his demeanor, I recognized what I had felt as a student—the need to examine, explore, and challenge assumptions critically. His questions forced me to ensure that my

101

lectures were clear and unambiguous. The young man's curiosity stimulated the two of us, as well as the rest of the class, to go beyond current understanding and to entertain alternative explanations for experimental observations. At the time I knew he was special. Today Dr. James Bennett is one of the most respected urologists in Atlanta. (A postscript to the story: Presently, Bennett is my urologist and performs my yearly prostrate examination. Prior to the exam, I always ask him, "I'm sure the biochemistry has progressed to the point that the finger exam is unnecessary." He always assures me, "Doc, you need to calm down and bend over.")

I recruited Dr. J. K. Haynes, from Meharry Medical College, to teach the new course in cell biology and direct the Office of Health Professions. Dr. Haynes was a Morehouse graduate with a PhD degree from Brown University. We renovated a laboratory on the second floor for his studies on sickle cells. Tom Blocker, a 1973 graduate of Morehouse, returned to the college as an assistant in the Office of Health Professions and lecturer in general biology. Later, as the Director of the Office of Health Professions, he contributed to Morehouse students going into the health professions in unparalleled numbers.

One summer we assembled a group of seniors from local high schools in a summer program designed to provide exposure to college-level courses and an introduction to careers in the sciences. A colleague, Dr. Carl Spight, and I experimented with teaching the process of creativity to the young group. To plan for the course, I visited Dr. E. Paul Torrence, professor at the University of Georgia, who was considered in academic circles to be the "Father of Creativity." He pioneered the development of the "benchmark method for quantifying creativity" and helped to shatter the theory that IQ tests alone were sufficient to gauge real intelligence. After our meeting in his office, Dr. Torrence encouraged us to use the tools he had developed, which included brainstorming techniques and modules designed to show students ways to approach problems creatively. His assessment procedure allowed instructors to award points on the quality of the creative approach and the solution. For example, students were asked to invent uses for a common item, such as a toy.

"How would you make this a better toy?" we might ask them. Or "How would you establish lunar colonies?" Student responses were evaluated for originality, number of ideas, flexibility (number of different categories), and elaboration of the ideas. We had fun with this class, and I regret that we did not incorporate this kind of approach into the biology department curriculum. The ability to innovate and the ability to think creatively are sought-after skills in today's technological environment.

Dr. Mapp obtained a grant to purchase an electron microscope for the department. The machine was his pride and joy. Unfortunately, the scope was seldom used. Later I hired a young PhD parasitologist, Dr. Betty Ruth Jones, who began to use the machine and offered the first course in electron microscopy to undergraduates. A cadre of undergraduate and graduate students worked with every member of the department. When we sponsored a day for poster session presentations for students engaged in research, very little wall space remained on the three floors in Hope Hall.

I knew that we would not have arrived as a research group until our experimentation and conclusions were published in a respected journal. Work toward the goal of publication was our number-one priority.

During the course of our investigations, we observed that nonreplicating and replicating forms of the plasmid DNA co-sedimented with the bacterial chromosome when the chromosome was preserved in its folded state. We also discovered that the replicating forms are preferentially associated with the folded chromosome structure. The finding was new, and we were the first to describe the phenomenon. We were anxious to publish the finding and worked diligently on the manuscript in preparation for submission to the *Journal of Bacteriology*.

Dr. Simon Silver, one of the editors of the *Journal*, submitted our paper for review. A few weeks later, I received a communication from him, saying that the reviewers had rejected our manuscript. I broke the news to Archibold and Clarence. We were devastated. Dr. Silver gave us the reviewer's comments, shared his personal observations, and encouraged us to resubmit. On the way home that evening,

I could not control the tears. I had convinced everyone that we could compete with the best laboratories in the world. The rejection was a refutation of my assertion. The next day, we had a meeting and decided not to be deterred. We repeated the experiments and answered all the questions the reviewers had raised. As we busily prepared our manuscript for resubmission to the *Journal*, I received an invitation to present our work on the international stage.

I suspect the invitation came as a result of the paper published with Novick in the *Journal of Molecular Biology*.

> Dear Dr. Sheehy,
>
> We would like to extend an invitation to you to present at the Third International Symposium on Antibiotic Resistance. Castle of Smolenice, Czechoslovakia, 1st-4th of June 1976. We will provide accommodations. You will be responsible for your travel. Please send the title of your talk to my attention. All manuscripts will be due in advance so as not to delay publication. If you accept this invitation, please advise as soon as possible.
>
> Sincerely,
> Professor L. Rosival, M.D.
> Czechoslovak Hygienic
> Society

What a break, I thought. All major laboratories conducting research on plasmids would be represented at the symposium. If I could attend, our work would earn worldwide attention. As arrangements for the trip to Soviet-occupied Czechoslovakia got underway, we worked to improve our results for resubmission to the *Journal*. However, the symposium was only months away, and I had not secured travel money, which would be approximately one thousand dollars. President Gloster appealed to Mr. Charles Merrill, trustee of the college, who agreed to provide the funds. Merrill had an interest in ways to improve relations between the United States and the communist bloc. The manuscript was proofed exhaustively by our brain trust, and slides were prepared. Saturday, the day before my departure, I received a check for a thousand dollars. However, I needed cash, and banks were not open on Saturdays. An appeal was made to Mr. Robert Paschal, a famous restaurateur in the area, who cashed the check.

Flying behind the Iron Curtain was a real adventure. Leaving from Atlanta, I changed planes in Germany for a shorter flight to Prague, Czechoslovakia. In Prague, I boarded a smaller, propeller-driven, Czechoslovak Airline plane to the city of Bratislava. A representative of the symposium met me on the tarmac, and within moments I was whisked away to a waiting car. The Castle of Smolenice, a short ride from the airport, is near the town of Smolenice. The castle was built in the fourteenth century and much later was converted into a conference center. I was assigned a room, which contained about ten individual beds. Tired from the long trip, I went to bed early. However, I was awakened about four o'clock in the morning by a knock at the door and a whisper that I had a phone call. I assumed that the message was a mistake. *Who would call me here?* I wondered, as I stumbled down a long staircase.

I picked up the phone. "Who is this?"

The answer was, "Did you call me?"

"Who is this? I repeated.

Although the connection was not very good, I heard, "This is Franca in Atlanta."

Ron Sheehy with Japanese Scientists

We resolved that the early hour (for me) was not the best time to talk and ended the call. Franca Elliott, my girlfriend, was the "girl next door." She was an accountant for the Medical Education Program, which would eventually become the Morehouse School of Medicine and was then located in a trailer next to my office. We were introduced by a mutual friend from India, Dr. Marimuthu, one of the first faculty members in the medical school, who thought of himself as quite a ladies' man. He had told me, "Ron, this is the girl for you. She is so beautiful." As it turned out, he was right. It was love at first sight, although I was careful to conceal the emotion. At that point in our lives, neither of us knew that this was the beginning of a long-term commitment.

The next day, as I prepared for my talk, several of the participants who had heard about the early morning call expressed concern. My presentation was groundbreaking and well-received. Attendees asked me to send reprints of our manuscript. In fact, the Director of the Career Development Award Program at the National Institutes of Health approached me after the talk. "Dr. Sheehy, I know you were turned down in the first round for this award, but I think you should reapply."

Considerable revelry took place in the castle bar that night. I was struck by the Japanese participants' high level of merriment. After more than a few drinks, we joined together and sang the anthem of the civil rights movement, "We Shall Overcome."

The return trip was more eventful than the trip to the conference. I left Czechoslovakia on a bus that traveled through the Iron Curtain. When the bus stopped at the checkpoint between Czechoslovakia and Austria, I saw the barbed wire and minefields that stretched for miles in both directions. I reflected that any form of oppression, whether apartheid in South Africa, southern-style segregation in America, or communist minefields, damages the human spirit.

When I arrived in Vienna, my first request was for a hot dog and a Coca-Cola. I checked into the Hotel Internationale. The next morning, I stepped out of the elevator door and discovered that the lobby was full of young black males. At first I thought I had flown back into the United States. Two travelling football teams from American universities had arrived to play an exhibition game in a stadium in Vienna. I accepted an invitation to join the teams on their bus and was treated as a member of the entourage. At the game, I was pressed into service on the sideline to translate the action on the field to the announcer, whose description was in German.

Back in Atlanta, I couldn't wait to tell the group of our success. We had persevered. Against the odds, we had prevailed. Our revised manuscript was mailed to Dr. Silver at the *Journal of Bacteriology* and was accepted in the first round of reviews. Our work was published in a major peer-reviewed journal, but that achievement was only the prelude. He also promised to use me as a reviewer for all manuscripts related to plasmid replication and folded chromosomes. Some time later, I received the proceedings of the conference in Czechoslovakia, "Plasmids: Medical and Theoretical Aspects," published by Springer-Verlag. I presented a copy to President Gloster as a gift, with a note to thank him for his support.

A few months later, I was invited to present at a conference, the *EMBO Workshop on Plasmids and Other Extrachromosomal Genetic Elements*, sponsored by the Max Planck Institute, in West Berlin. The letter of invitation from the organizers assured me that all expenses would be paid by the Institute. With the exception of the plenary talks, invited participants prepared posters that displayed their research results, which was not unusual for a conference. The organizers of the conference were sensitive to my being the only African American and made a point to invite me to all of their social gatherings. I politely turned down a few of the invitations, however, since I wanted my mother and sister Ronetta to enjoy the trip as well. We took some sight-seeing tours in West Berlin and went on an excursion to East Germany through the Berlin Wall. During our trip to East Germany, my mother argued with a cashier about correct change, even though the exchange from dollars to deutschmarks was complicated. She had lived up to her nickname, "Dollar." I gently reminded her that we were behind the Iron Curtain and on the communist side of the border.

I had seen the barriers erected by the communist state in Czechoslovakia; however, the Berlin Wall was more imposing and formidable. A testament to the human spirit's drive for freedom occurred in 1989 when the Berlin Wall, which symbolized the Iron Curtain between Western Europe and the Eastern communist bloc, was dismantled.

Archibold accepted an invitation to present our work at the *NATO Conference on the Biology of Bacterial Plasmids*, held in Athens, Greece. We had successfully achieved recognition for our research at an unlikely starting point, Morehouse College, a small, historically black college. We had demonstrated that a competitive laboratory could be established at Morehouse, just as I had believed. We designed the physical facilities, built the organizational infrastructure, sustained economic resources, eventually raised over ten million dollars, and maintained a sufficient level of inventiveness and creativity to accomplish research goals. This level of achievement at a black college is the best argument for the significant contributions to scientific discovery that can result when essential resources are available at similar institutions.

It was my good fortune that Judy Bender, an instructor in the department, expressed a desire to pursue the PhD degree. I agreed to be her thesis advisor. Judy, like other whites who taught at Morehouse, had decided to make a contribution to black higher education. For Judy's research, we renovated another laboratory on the first floor with funding provided by the Environmental Protection Agency. Judy's thesis research employed a bacterial detection system to evaluate carcinogens in the water supply. Judy eventually received her PhD degree from Atlanta University and subsequently established the first course in environmental biology in the department.

We decided to attend one of the regional meetings of the American Society of Microbiology in Tampa. The four of us— Archibald, Clarence, Judy, and I—drove down. On the way, we joked about three black guys and a white woman driving to Florida in 1977 and the possible repercussions if we were stopped by the police. Fortunately, our worst fears were not realized, and we arrived in Tampa safely. Clarence and Judy presented our research, and we gathered for a party at my parents' house after the sessions were concluded. John Betz, whom I had not seen in years, was at the meeting, and I invited him to the party. He wanted to know how we were able to do our level of experimentation at a small black college. His question was legitimate, and without a hint of smugness, I assured him of our state-of-the-art operation.

Every year we participated in the regional meetings of the American Society for Microbiology. We began to use the meetings as a forum to introduce our graduate and undergraduate students to the world of science beyond Morehouse. The events also produced an audience for presentations of research findings that had not reached the stage for publication. I remember a meeting, sponsored by the University of Florida in Gainesville, where we collectively submitted more papers for presentations than any of the other colleges or universities represented. Another memorable meeting of the Society was held in Birmingham, Alabama. Roy Curtiss had left Oak Ridge and was a distinguished professor at the Dental School at the University of Alabama in Birmingham.

I arranged for our fairly large contingent of undergraduates and graduate students to visit his laboratory before we left Birmingham. When we filed into Curtiss's lab, he was astonished at our numbers. I could not have been more pleased with the excitement and enthusiasm of my colleagues and students.

In 1978 I was asked to serve on the Microbial Genetics Review Group at the National Institutes of Health (NIH). While inclusiveness, diversity, and affirmative action were wrapped in the logic of the invitation, the appointment was, nevertheless, a coveted assignment. All proposals in the field of microbial genetics, submitted to the NIH for funding, were reviewed by the panel. Luther Williams was already a member of the panel, which consisted of no more than twelve members. Two African Americans in the esteemed group represented a remarkable coincidence. Every four months, I received a box of proposals for evaluation. In advance of the meeting in Washington, I prepared critical reviews of each proposal, which I defended at the meeting. I was privy to ideas and research findings that emanated from the most important investigators in the country. On one occasion, I was assigned a proposal for continued funding from Dr. Jane Setlow, with whom I had a lab rotation at Oak Ridge and who had suggested that I consider a different career path. The irony of this was not lost on me, and I spent considerable time reviewing her proposal, which was brilliant, as was all of her work. I made suggestions for improvement, which I presented to the panel. Dr. Setlow's proposal was approved. The work of the committee was intellectually stimulating, and I enjoyed every minute of it. My involvement with the molecular genetics panel ended after I received a request from the National Cancer Institute.

The staff person assigned to the Clinical Cancer Program Project and Cancer Center Support Review Committee at the National Cancer Institute (NCI) called. He asked if I would accept a three-year appointment to the committee. The panel supervised funding for all cancer centers in the country. Since I was a basic scientist and my research was not directly related to cancer, I was surprised to be selected.

My first meeting in Washington was an eye-opener. I was the only person of color in a group of about twenty. The NCI committee clearly needed diversity. Moreover, the African American community required special involvement in cancer research, since specific cancers—prostate and certain breast cancers—are prevalent in its population. The committee convened three times a year in Washington; committee members were also frequently asked to travel for site visits around the country. I remember a site visit in which a scientist who investigated lung cancer showed contrasting slides of lung tissue from a smoker and a nonsmoker. The smoker's lung tissue was black and deformed, whereas the nonsmoker's tissue was pink, its normal color, and healthy in appearance. I had been a smoker for twenty years, but after that visit, I committed to stop smoking. Within days, I stopped cold turkey. I have not smoked a cigarette since that time.

During the years of my appointment, 1979–1981, I visited many of the major cancer centers in the United States. The meetings in Washington, as well as the site visits, were solitary affairs for me. Most of the time, I was the only African American among the visiting evaluators as well as the resident scientists and administrators. Morehouse provided a psychological anchor for my forays into the white scientific establishment. The paucity of African Americans in cancer research was conspicuous. On one occasion, I was assigned to a team responsible for review of the cancer center at the predominantly black Howard University Medical School. In my view, the Howard Cancer Center was underfunded, considering the extensive prevalence of cancer in the black community, particularly in Washington, D.C. An unexplained epidemic of prostate cancer occurred among black men in the Capital City. I strongly supported the grant and advocated for increases in funds during the site visit and at the committee meeting in Washington. I concluded my term with great respect for research efforts throughout the country—both basic and clinical—in the enormous endeavors that are underway to understand and cure this disease.

Undergraduates at Morehouse reaped the benefits of my association with the review committees. Students discussed and analyzed research findings in cancer molecular biology years before the information reached the textbooks or the general public. Two additional postdoctoral fellows joined the laboratory: Dr. Elaine Davis, who had recently received her PhD degree from the Meharry Medical College in Nashville, and Dr. Lycurgus Muldrow, who had recently received his PhD degree from the Graduate School of Biomedical Sciences at Oak Ridge. Both were well-trained and immediately took individual projects to investigate aspects of plasmid molecular biology.

Ron and Franca

After a fairly lengthy courtship, I proposed to Franca in 1981. My procrastination bordered on foolhardiness. When her Aunt Eoline heard of the proposal, her first comment was, "It's about time." I initially thought we would have a small wedding in the Danforth Chapel on campus, a space with a seating capacity around fifty. Franca's ideas were quite different, and our wedding eventually drew more than four hundred well-wishers.

A small college that could house a research group with the personnel and capability we assembled at Morehouse was unusual. While we enjoyed support from the administration, the officials had no idea of the scope or extensiveness of the research. Tensions eventually developed around the role of research versus our mission to teach undergraduates. Fortunately we demonstrated, to the satisfaction of the administration, that our undergraduates were well-served by the emphasis on research in the department.

In the laboratory, a multiplicity of projects involving numerous aspects of plasmid biology in different organisms ran simultaneously. Our core research remained centered around the earlier observation of the co-sedimentation of nonreplicating and replicating forms of plasmid DNA with the folded chromosome. We turned our attention to determining the intracellular location of the molecules. After months of research, primarily through the efforts of Errol Archibold, his student Jerry Wilson, and David Allison from Oak Ridge, who assisted with the electron microscopy, we published the results in the *Journal of Bacteriology*. The title and abstract at the top of the first page of the journal article read as follows:

Membrane-Bound Fractions of R6K Plasmid DNA in Escherichia coli

Errol R. Archibold, Jerry D. Wilson, David P. Allison, and Ronald J. Sheehy

Department of Biology, Morehouse College, Atlanta, Georgia

Received 3 March 1983/Accepted 7 August 1983

The intracellular location of plasmid DNA has been of interest in an effort to understand the maintenance of these molecules. We have employed a simple procedure which enables us to isolate from exponentially grown cells on sucrose gradients membrane complexed forms of R6K plasmid DNA. Electron micrographs identified the complexing of membrane fractions to circular forms of R6K DNA. Biochemical studies of the complexed R6K molecules showed the presence of membrane-specific proteins and suggested that complexing of R6K DNA was primarily with inner membrane fractions of *Escherichia coli*.

The value of the work was our contribution to growing evidence that bacterial plasmids associate with the bacterial membrane for plasmid maintenance and for replication. We had not answered all questions that concerned plasmid replication and maintenance, but we had reached a milestone in our work. We had not discovered a major cure for a disease or developed a patent for a new invention, but we had added to the storehouse of human knowledge in an important area of molecular biology.

I was extremely proud of my association with the students, both undergraduates and graduates, and my colleagues, who contributed to the explosion of research activity in the department of biology at Morehouse College during the '70s and early '80s. Upon reflection, we were successful because we dared to believe that we were not constrained by personal limitations and that we could succeed through our own hard work, inventiveness, and creativity.

Morehouse Research Group and Faculty

Epilogue: The Funeral

Gathered in the backyard, we sat on old makeshift wooden benches, as men did on such occasions. My grandfather, "Papa," had died. I was the first to discover him on Christmas day, the morning of his passing.

Mr. Stephen "Papa" Hart

I was in a pensive mood as we traded stories of our childhood. I recalled our family dinners with Papa at the head of the table. He seldom asked for the chicken to be passed his way, but simply raised up from his chair at the end of the table, lunged toward the plate of chicken, and speared his favorite piece. I made a mistake and asked my grandmother why he did that, and she quickly hushed me.

After dinner she told me, "Ronald, he buys the chicken, and he can stick a fork in it if it pleases him."

I shared memories of evenings when, as a youngster, I joined my grandmother on the front porch to wait on his return from work. We traded stories, especially about "Uncle Bubba," one of my mother's brothers: how determined he was that my cousin, Roland,

and I would do our math homework; how he had discovered that his grandfather, Martin Hart, was buried in the white cemetery, and that he had left his job as a teacher in Sebring, Florida, rather than to change a grade for a student at the insistence of the white superintendent.

Cousin Jackie's husband, Bernard Lemon, listened. He was not particularly talkative. I knew he was a part-time singer in nightclubs in central Florida, where they lived, and I inquired about the progress of his singing career.

"Well, Bernard, I know you are knocking them dead with that voice of yours."

"No, Ronald," he said, with a serious expression. "I've decided to drop singing and become a minister."

The news was a shock, and I didn't want to create an embarrassing moment with an obvious question. Before we left, I asked him what had brought about the change. He said, "It was something I have been thinking about for some time, but there is a book I read that sort of sealed the deal for me."

"What is this book?" I asked.

Midway Church

"The author's name is Taylor Caldwell, and the title is *Dialogues with the Devil*. I have a copy in the car," he said, and he turned to get the book out of his glove compartment. Reverend Bernard Lemon is now a Presiding Elder over the Lakeland Florida District in the AME Church.

The funeral was a sad occasion. Our family gathered at Mother Midway Church for the service. I listened to the eulogies, which I could barely hear above the sobs in the sanctuary. My grandfather was a beloved member of the church and one of its oldest members. I boarded the plane back to Atlanta in a somber, reflective mood. The book was in my coat pocket, and as I settled in my seat, I began to read.

"There is no end of knowledge in Heaven, no end of learning. The soul pursues new knowledge and learns forever. It does not stand like a marble confronting changelessness. Its face is eternally lit with the fires and the colors of new universes and new aspirations and new adventures. It clamors to know. Yet it can never know completely, and that is its reward. God is like an earthly father who constantly places new riddles before his children, and who smiles as they eagerly guess its secrets and learn its answers. There are always new books to read, new wonders to excite the imagination, new vistas to explore."

I bent over in my seat to hide the tears that streamed down my face. My heart had been touched. I thought about my deepest desires. I thought about the science fair ... Victor ... my days as a student at Morehouse ... my long hours in the lab at Oak Ridge and New York ... and my return to Morehouse. These life-altering events seemed to stream before my consciousness. In the passage, I found a spiritual dimension to my quest that I had previously ignored. "No disturbing variety, no uncertainty, no danger, and no test of courage, no challenge, and no enigmas," was Caldwell's description of hell. She writes that heaven, by contrast, "is where the soul pursues new knowledge and learns forever." I now believe that the desire to inquire, question, and explore was not mine to claim as an individual, but emanated from the source of everything, God. It is God's plan for us to probe, to inquire, to explore, to solve riddles of our world and universe. It is our responsibility to improve the mind to meet the challenge and fulfill our destiny.